Suffering

Banner Mini-Guides introduce the reader to some of the major themes and issues related to the Christian faith. They lay a solid foundation of Bible teaching while encouraging more thorough exploration of the theme with suggestions for further reading. The mini-guides will seamlessly fit into the teaching quarters of the church year with their thirteen-chapter format, making them useful for group as well as for individual study.

Suffering

God's Purpose in Our Pain

Banner Mini-Guides
Christian Living

Paul D. Wolfe

THE BANNER OF TRUTH TRUST

THE BANNER OF TRUTH TRUST

Head Office
3 Murrayfield Road
Edinburgh, EH12 6EL
UK

North America Office
610 Alexander Spring Road
Carlisle, PA 17015
USA

banneroftruth.org

ISBN
Print: 978 1 80040 364 2
Epub: 978 1 80040 365 9
Kindle: 978 1 80040 366 6

*

Typeset in 10/14 pt Minion Pro
at the Banner of Truth Trust, Edinburgh

Printed in the USA by
Versa Press, Inc.,
East Peoria, IL

To Dr Richard B. Gaffin, Jr.

The truth of the Christian's union with Christ runs through this book like a thread. I trust I got that truth from the Bible, and not ultimately from any mere man. But Dr Gaffin, more than anyone else in my life, is the mere man who helped me get it. And he's done so, not only by his teaching and writing, but also by his example. Dr Gaffin has known suffering of his own, and has shown many, including myself, what it looks like to follow Christ through the valley.

In memory of Dr Howard Griffith

Howard learned much from Dr Gaffin too. Howard spent a lifetime humbly and lovingly sharing with others what he learned from God's word. Countless lives were touched by his own: church members and seminary students, family and friends, next-door neighbours and perfect strangers. While I was writing this book Howard was suffering from cancer, and he did so with a shining faith. Now the book is done, and Howard's suffering is too, and his faith has given way to sight. And Jesus is not ashamed to call him 'brother.'

Contents

1

Getting Our Bearings

There are two types of books they say you should never write: books on parenting, and books on suffering. Books on parenting, because then you and your children feel like bugs under a microscope, and people who know you say, 'Are you kidding me? *He* wrote a book on parenting? Please!' And books on suffering, because then you feel like you've certainly signed yourself up for a good bruising during the writing process, so the book you're writing has a ring of truth, or after it's published, so you're given plenty of opportunity to apply what you've just written. And I suppose some weary parents would say, 'Parenting and suffering. What's the difference?' (I wouldn't. I love being a dad. My children are great. But I can imagine. I've heard stories.)

Undaunted, I wrote this book anyway, a book about suffering. And why? Well, I wrote it because I know I'm in God's hands, that's why. The Christian is set free from the shackles of paralyzing fear—including any superstitious fear of *What Might Happen to Me if I Do This or That*—and what has set him free is the knowledge that absolutely nothing can cut him off from the love of God in Christ Jesus his Lord (Rom. 8:38, 39). I think often of Psalm 112 and what it says about the righteous man who fears God: 'He is not afraid of bad news; his heart is firm, trusting in the Lord' (verse 7).

Though every Christian on earth remains a work in progress, needing to grow further in righteousness and reverent fear and firm trust, still that's comfort every Christian can take personally: I don't have to fear bad news, not because bad news is impossible for the Christian—it certainly isn't, as we'll see—but because the good news of the gospel is so much stronger than the worst bad news we might ever get. And even the bad news that comes my way will have been appointed for me by a Father who loves me, and who's using it to bring about 'an eternal weight of glory beyond all comparison' (2 Cor. 4:17). So we can confidently battle back against the superstitions that would keep us silent, afraid to speak. We can raise our battle flag and unsheathe our sword and shout, 'Away with fear!' And then start writing.

Stirred up by way of reminder

And then as soon as you start writing, another realization hits home, and hits hard: you've taken on a topic that the human race has been wrestling with, and talking about, from time immemorial! We all know there's no shortage of books out there on the subject of suffering, books ancient and modern, and that does give you pause as you pick up your pen to write another one. (You glance up at your bookshelves, and giants of faith and philosophy are looking back down at you saying, 'Yes, we've written on that subject too. We look forward to reviewing your manuscript.') I vividly recall a conversation I had years ago with an older, wiser Christian. I phoned him when I was contemplating writing a book about suffering I'd experienced and lessons learned along the way. In that conversation I expressed this very reservation—'there are plenty of books about suffering; does the world really need another one?'—and the answer I got back was gold. He said, 'There may be thousands of books about suffering, but there are billions of sufferers. Write it.' So I did,[1] and now I'm at it again.

Of course, this is true of nearly every subject, and not just suffering. There are several reasons why it pays to re-cover well-covered ground. First of all, as Peter puts it (twice) in his second epistle, we can all afford to be 'stirred up by way of reminder' (2 Pet. 1:13; 3:1). Have you ever noticed how frequently, and naturally, Christians tend to express their appreciation for a sermon they've heard or a book or article they've read by calling it a wholesome 'reminder' of truths they've heard before? And rightly so. If this book you're reading right now proves a blessing in your life, the benefit may very well be of that character—a reminder. You've likely heard before that the Lord reigns

---

[1] *My God Is True: Lessons Learned along Cancer's Dark Road* (Edinburgh: Banner of Truth Trust, 2009).

over our trials (see chapter 5), and that he brings them to pass to make us more like Christ (chapter 6), and that one day all our trials will end (chapter 12). I freely admit, I'm not saying anything particularly earth-shattering in this book! Keep reading anyway: the Lord is pleased to stir us up by way of reminder. This is perhaps especially true when it comes to suffering: our trials can have the effect of shaking and dislodging in our souls the very truths that enable us to endure—and that can happen even if we've been steeped in those truths for a long, long time. Sometimes what we need more than anything else is that friendly reminder: a fellow believer comes along and says just what we need to hear so as to put those truths back in place, at a time when we may not be in the best shape to do it ourselves. Dislodged no longer.

Second of all, each new articulation of Christian truth comes to us from the peculiar personal vantage point of the speaker or writer, shaped by their experiences, couched in their vocabulary, expressive of their generation, and then it touches down in our lives against the backdrop of who we are and what we're going through at the time. The writing-and-reading of a book turns out to be a remarkably personal and punctual form of human interaction, even if the author and reader never meet. Indeed, even if you order the book online! This is why the very same book might bless you in a way it doesn't help another person, or in a way it didn't help you three years ago. We end up reminded, but also reminded in a fresh way, thanks to some other voice, and right on time. The same Lord who reigns over our pains also reigns over the helps he brings our way so that we can make sense of those pains, and make the most of them. His timing is always impeccable, and his remedies are too.

Human experiences, divine word

I should also say I offer this book keenly aware of the fact that, because of my own current health and wealth and race and place and, well, timing (it's the twenty-first century, after all, and not, say, the eleventh), I have been personally spared depths of suffering that fellow human beings (Christian and non-Christian alike) have had to undergo throughout the ages and are currently undergoing around the world. I've traversed my own valleys, to be sure, but many others have had to go into deeper, darker places.

But I've been reminded that the only life we can live is the life that God has actually appointed for us, that is, for each one of us individually, and that it's unreasonable to expect anyone to be moulded by the sorrows of others (and their blessings too) as if he himself had experienced them firsthand. True, we are called to share in others' joys and sorrows: the Bible says, 'Rejoice with those who rejoice, weep with those who weep' (Rom. 12:15). That's what it means to be empathetic. But even at its best, even at its most intimate, the joy or sorrow we feel in solidarity with another is at least a few steps removed from what they themselves are feeling. (And oftentimes it's many more than just a few steps. Oftentimes we're miles away, in spite of our best and most compassionate efforts to listen and understand and enter in.) There is something inescapably individual and unique and uncommon about each person's experiences, whether bitter or blessed. As the wise man teaches us, 'The heart knows its own bitterness, and no stranger shares its joy' (Prov. 14:10).

But here's the point: that reality shouldn't render us silent about our experiences, since that would mean no one could ever get wisdom from anyone else! Though my experiences may not match yours, or his, or hers, or theirs, still what pains me is my suffering, and what thrills me is my joy—whether major or minor, however lasting or fleeting, whether shocking or standard—and what I've learned from it is still worth sharing (and so is what you've learned from yours). We shouldn't feel guilty because we haven't tasted everything that others have known before us and around us, or fear that we have nothing valuable to say. Who knows? We may actually find in our relationships with dear friends and in our encounters with perfect strangers that we have lessons to teach and learn that would surprise us and them!

In any case, what matters most is not what any of us has experienced, but what God has spoken in his word. Our personal experiences, when used wisely, are so many windows on that divine message. And on this subject—on the subject of suffering in the Christian life—it turns out God has said quite a bit. So let's make that our aim in these pages: to learn from the God who made us, and who rules over us, even over our pains, and who's given us a Saviour who suffered on our behalf to give us the hope of a new world in which books like this one won't have to be written anymore. I'm glad I got to write this book, truly … but I can't wait for that world. How about you?

2

The Suffering Servant

It is well known as the shortest verse in the Bible.

'Jesus wept.'

That's John 11:35.

But did you know there's another verse in the Bible—this one not quite so short—which tells us that Jesus wept … *loudly*?

'In the days of his flesh, Jesus offered up prayers and supplications, with loud cries and tears, to him who was able to save him from death, and he was heard because of his reverence.'

That's Hebrews 5:7.

What the writer of Hebrews is describing in that one not-so-short verse is Jesus' experience as a man who suffered in this life, including the anticipation of the end of his life on the cross. And what the writer is teaching us there is that Jesus suffered as a man of prayer, and lamentation, and trust. The prayers he prayed, his Father heard and honoured, because the Father looked upon his beloved

Son as the reverent servant he truly was. Jesus' prayers in the Garden of Gethsemane the night before he died rightly come to mind, but the time frame the author has in view is apparently broader than that one night: he's describing something that was true of our Saviour 'in the days of his flesh,' that is, throughout the time of his earthly life, and he goes on in the next verse (verse 8) to speak of Jesus' extended experience of suffering as that which made him the complete Saviour we needed him to be.

Admittedly, we might find it jarring to read in Scripture that Jesus wept loudly. Sometimes when we picture somebody crying like that (or we exhibit such expression ourselves), what comes to mind is somebody who's out of control, somebody who's undone and unravelled by his pains, somebody who's lost perspective. 'If he were more composed,' we might think, 'more dignified, more clear-eyed, more faithful, surely the volume of his weeping would be somewhere in the neighbourhood of Medium instead of High. The dial turned to five instead of eleven.'

And to be honest, we picture that because sometimes it's true: it's sometimes the case among sinners that our weeping does reflect a certain lack of control and perspective and trust in God. So when we consider the Son of God, of all people, offering up prayers and supplications with cries and tears, we might imagine the sort of muted, mid-range emotional expression that wouldn't make anyone else in the room feel—uncomfortable. After all, he *is* the Son of God, and so he, of all people, was self-controlled and dignified and clear-eyed and faithful. Surely that means Jesus felt only Medium pain, and therefore cried only Medium tears.

But it was not so. If anything, the fact that Jesus was fully divine and sinlessly human means he felt what he felt more intensely, and not less. And why? Because Jesus, more than anyone else who ever lived, before or since, felt in the depths of his soul the discrepancy between the way things actually are in this cursed world, and the way things would have been apart from sin, and will be in the world to come. We are the ones whose souls can be calloused and numb. His was not. His was sensitive and alert and alive. When he was pained, he felt it profoundly, and he expressed it accordingly.

We can put it this way. Jesus loved God in the way that he suffered and wept. It was an expression of his love and devotion and faithfulness to his Father, and not a blemish on it. Which means that he suffered and wept with all his heart and soul and mind and strength. We don't know what Jesus looked like, or sounded like, or how many decibels he reached when he cried, which is okay, because we don't need to. But this much we do know: Jesus felt pain deeply, and he wept loudly. He wasn't limited by our notions of Medium.

Sorrowful man, beloved servant

We shouldn't be surprised to find in the New Testament that Jesus suffered a wide variety of pains and sorrows, and prayed accordingly. After all, the Old Testament anticipated the day when a Saviour would come who would be just such a man as that. Hundreds of years before Jesus was born, the prophet Isaiah foretold his coming as one who would be 'despised and rejected by men, a man of sorrows, and acquainted with grief' (Isa. 53:3). Jesus' experience in this world proved Isaiah's words true.

But we need to notice that Isaiah foretold another side of the story as well. Yes, the figure anticipated in Isaiah chapter 53 would taste sorrows and griefs, but that same person is described by God himself at the outset of the passage as 'my servant' (52:13). And that same servant has already been introduced to us in Isaiah—again, introduced by God himself—as one 'whom I uphold, my chosen, in whom my soul delights' (42:1). Put these various pieces together, and we come to a striking and important conclusion: the fact that Jesus suffered as he did was no indication that God didn't love him (if you'll pardon the double negative). To the contrary, Jesus tasted sorrows and griefs as God's beloved servant, in whom the Father delighted. Indeed, it must have been the knowledge of his Father's love for him that sustained him in those very sorrows.

Sorrowful man. Beloved servant. Same person.

Our Christ connection

Once we consider Christ's experience in this way, we have to see ourselves in the same light. God's word is unmistakably clear: the followers of the suffering servant can expect to suffer themselves. Jesus himself warned his disciples to expect opposition to their ministry, and then he backed it up with this broad, abiding principle: 'A disciple is not above his teacher, nor a servant above his master' (Matt. 10:24). Christians who expect a pain-free Christian life are putting themselves above their Master. And that is one place where they certainly do not belong, a position they may not occupy.

And this particular servant-master relationship is unlike any other. We who believe in Jesus are joined to our Master-Saviour in a faith-union that is most intimate, to the point that the New Testament piles up prepositional expressions in order to capture it: by faith we are in Christ, and Christ is in us, because Christ's Spirit is in us, and we are in the Spirit, and we believe 'into' Christ, and so forth. For a sampler read Paul's glorious run-on praise-sentence that is Ephesians 1:3-14 (and yes, in Paul's original Greek those twelve verses are one long sentence) and count the instances of union-with-Christ language as you go. Those instances number in the double digits—just in that one sentence! The New Testament's testimony is rich and rewarding: by faith we are found in Christ so that we receive the benefits of his saving work, and become his brothers and sisters in the family of God, and come to life with his resurrection life, and share in his sufferings, but also share in his hope that one day our suffering will end and give way to glory instead. To borrow Paul's language from another setting, we can say that the Christian 'lives and moves and has his being' in Jesus.

That's why this book about suffering in the Christian life begins with Christ himself. We'll only grasp the Bible's teaching on this topic if the cross of Christ (and all the crosses he bore leading up to that last one) are close at hand. Christ's pattern was suffering-unto-glory ('Was it not necessary that the Christ should suffer these things and enter into his glory?'—Luke 24:26), and therefore so is ours (we are 'heirs of God and fellow heirs with Christ, provided we suffer with him in order that we may also be glorified with him'—Rom 8:17). This is why Paul can say that he wants to know Christ and 'share his sufferings' (Phil. 3:10). This is why Paul can describe his own apostolic hardships as 'filling up what is lacking in Christ's afflictions' (Col. 1:24). This is why Peter can say to suffering Christians that they shouldn't be surprised by what they're experiencing, counselling them instead to 'rejoice insofar as you share Christ's sufferings' (1 Pet. 4:13). In this book you're reading we begin with Christ, the one to whom we are united by faith, because that's the only way fully to make sense of our own experience and to glorify the one who is Jesus' Father and ours, Jesus' God and ours.

A pronunciation guide

With that aim in view, let me offer this little bit of pronunciation advice. We've considered the sufferings of Jesus as point #1 in a book about the Christian life. Notice that adjective: the 'Christian' life. Followers of Jesus have been called 'Christians' since the beginning of the apostle Paul's ministry in Antioch (Acts 11:26). Of course, they were called that (likely by outside observers, and perhaps by sneering opponents) because of their association with the one they believed to be the Christ of God. And remember what the title 'Christ' means: it means 'Anointed One,' as does 'Messiah.' To call Jesus 'the Christ' is to affirm that he was immeasurably anointed, or endowed, with the Holy Spirit for the work his Father had given him to do, which was to save his people from their sins by his life, death, and resurrection. (Isaiah anticipated this too, by the way: the prophet records God's suffering servant saying, 'The Spirit of the Lord God is upon me, because the Lord has anointed me to bring good news to the poor,' 61:1). So it's a potent title, 'Christ.' Which is why it loomed so large in the way his first followers thought about him, and trusted in him, and worshipped him, that they were given the label 'Christians' by those who got to know what this new movement was all about.

Now, consider this point about pronunciation. Is it not unfortunate that we always pronounce the nickname 'Christian' with a short 'i' sound, so that it *doesn't* sound like the title 'Christ'? Because of the way we pronounce it, the association between *Christ* Jesus and his followers which the nickname was meant to capture is diminished in our minds, if not lost altogether. Don't get me wrong: I have friends named 'Chris' and a best friend named 'Christy' and I'm grateful for all of them (especially the latter). But if we always pronounce our nickname 'Christian' with a short 'i' so that it sounds like 'Chris' or 'Christy' or 'fist' or 'list' or 'mist' (you get the gist), then we miss out on the force of that term. So here's my advice: every once in a while, Christian, call yourself a 'Chrīst-ian'—say it with a long 'i' sound—and let that sink in. It will sound funny, I know.

It sounds funny to my ears too. But that's precisely why it's such a valuable exercise. Call yourself a 'Chrīst-ian,' and let that funny, awkward sound remind you that everything you are, and have, and experience, and endure, and suffer (emphasis here on 'suffer') is true of you now in union with Jesus who is the Christ, the Messiah, the Anointed One of God, the beloved servant of God in whom his soul delights.

Where we go from here

The truth of the Christian's union with Christ isn't just the first point in this book. It's the overarching point we'll take with us through the rest of this book. The other truths we'll consider as we make our way (the reality of suffering, the purposes of suffering, the end of suffering, and more) all bring us back to Christ in some way or another, and to the reality that believers are in him, and he in us.

So if somebody sees you reading this book and asks, 'What are you reading?', you can say, 'I'm reading a book about the Chrīst-ian life.' Say it like that. Pronounce it like that. Long 'i' sound. And if they say, 'That sounds funny,' maybe you'll say, 'It does, doesn't it? But it's growing on me.'

3

The Reality of Suffering

In the early centuries of the Christian church, orthodox theologians found themselves combating a wide variety of 'isms' that countered biblical truth about God and Jesus. (At least, we call them 'isms' now.) One of those strands of thought came to be known as 'Docetism,' from the Greek verb *dokeō*, meaning 'to think or seem.' The hallmark of Docetism was the idea that Jesus of Nazareth wasn't really a man: he just seemed to be a man. It just looked that way. Some who claimed to be Christian claimed this about Christ because they considered it an impossibility that the Son of God should actually truly take to himself a human nature like our own, and then experience its limitations. They may have thought they were honouring the Son by guarding him against such a demeaning doctrine as the Incarnation (they considered it demeaning, I mean), but of course they were *dis*-honouring him instead, fashioning their own pre-conceived notions of what's possible for a divine person to do and then allowing those notions to rule out what the Bible clearly rules in. When Paul calls Jesus 'the man Christ Jesus' (1 Tim. 2:5), he means it. When the writer of Hebrews says that the Son 'partook of flesh and blood' so as 'to be made like his brothers in every respect' (2:14, 17), he means it. As the Westminster Confession of Faith puts it, the Son of God was willing to 'take upon him man's nature, with all the essential properties, and common infirmities thereof, yet without sin' (WCF 8.2).

The error of Docetism (denying Jesus' true humanity) and the countering truth of Scripture (affirming his humanity instead) have much to do with the subject of suffering. It is a Docetic tendency, if not an outright tenet, to baulk at the thought that the Son of God might experience real pain and cry out to God about it. And it is precisely that discomfort which we need to address. We need to be clear: the Son of God wasn't play-acting when he wept. He wasn't pretending to be pained, merely finding a way to manufacture tears from his eyes like a skilled actor on the stage, all the while needing to ask his director, 'Tell me again, what's my motivation here?' We need to be clear: his sufferings were real. So was his inward pain. So were his anguished prayers.

The spectrum of his sufferings

As we saw in chapter 2, the prophet Isaiah looked forward to the day when a saviour would come who would be 'despised and rejected by men, a man of sorrows, and acquainted with grief' (Isa. 53:3). The portrait of Jesus painted by the New Testament Gospel-writers fills out that simple prophetic pencil line with vivid colours.

Jesus' sufferings ran the gamut. For example, he suffered as a servant of God who was opposed by those who were opposed to God, or who at least didn't understand God's purposes the way he did. Read through the Gospels and note the relentless opposition and persecution he endured—and sometimes opposition and misunderstanding from his own disciples. Matthew's Gospel account alone provides quite a sampler. In one passage the Pharisees are calling him a friend of demons for healing people (9:32-34); in another passage two of his disciples and their mother come to him asking for greatness because they don't understand what true greatness amounts to (20:20-28). In one passage Satan is tempting him over and over again when he's hungry and spent (4:1-11); in another Peter is rebuking him, Satan-like, for his determination to die on the cross (16:21-23). In one passage his disciples are abandoning him to be arrested alone, in the dark (27:47-56); in another, Roman soldiers are shedding his blood with Roman nails pounded through his flesh into a Roman cross, while watchers and passers-by mock and revile him (27:32-44). Jesus suffered as a servant of God because he lived and laboured among those who were not, or who failed to understand what true kingdom service amounts to.

But Jesus also suffered as a man living in this cursed world. In other words, he had to endure the sorts of pains and inconveniences that were (and remain) common for the human race, experienced by those who know God and those who don't. Pains felt in his body, frustration experienced in his work, alienation arising in his relationships. All of these things Jesus handled without sin, but handle them he did. Again, consider the testimony of the Westminster Confession of Faith: the Son '[took] upon him man's nature, with all the essential properties, and common infirmities thereof, yet without sin' (WCF 8.2). Notice: 'common infirmities.' Uncommon though Jesus himself was in a host of ways, still we have in him a high priest 'who in every respect has been tempted as we are, yet without sin' (Heb. 4:15). Had he been immune to the common infirmities and difficulties and trials of human life in this world, then he would cease to be a Saviour who was tempted as we are in every way.

Now, to be well rounded in our thinking, we need to acknowledge that Jesus' earthly life wasn't unbroken and unmitigated misery from beginning to end. Though he was 'a man of sorrows, and acquainted with grief,' he also was a man of many blessings, and acquainted with joy: he knew the joys of family and friendship, and the blessings of work and play, and the joys of worship and service. His human experience was thorough human experience, and our Christology should be just as thorough. But our main point here is clear enough: he did taste sorrows and griefs, and not just at the end of his life, but throughout it. How could he not, living as true man in a painful world, living as devoted Son in a God-opposing world?

Our spectrum too

Observing this truth about Jesus pays off because it teaches us not to be surprised when we find that the same thing is true of us. Like the Christ, we who are Chrīst-ians can expect to encounter both kinds of difficulties in this world: those that are directly attributable to our faith, but also those that belong to human experience in general.

On the one hand, there is suffering that's traceable to our being Christians. As Paul warned Timothy, 'all who desire to live a godly life in Christ Jesus will be persecuted' (2 Tim. 3:12). This is due to the fact that we're living as those committed to God and his gospel in a world in which most people remain opposed to them, and who therefore find themselves implicitly (and uncomfortably) judged by our testimony. And that persecution itself runs the gamut: everything from outright hostility to snide sarcasm to subtle opposition. As Charles Spurgeon once commented, 'If we cannot be torn in pieces by the roaring lion, we may be hugged to death by the bear. The devil cares very little which it is, as long as he destroys our love for Christ and our confidence in him.'

There are Christian pastors who find themselves in prison for preaching Christ. And then their imprisonment ends in martyrdom, leaving wives and children and churches behind. There are Christian college students whose professors seem to target them for the rest of the semester after their faith is made known. And then some dorm-mates do the same. There are Christian wives who endure the daily mockery of their husbands after the wives come to faith in Jesus. And the mockery only seems to increase in bitterness over time. Persecution takes all of these forms and more.

On the other hand, Christians are not exempt from the sorts of trials that everybody has to deal with, whether they know Christ or not. Illnesses that ravage the body. Misunderstandings that break up relationships. Injustice at the hands of earthly powers. Ruin at the hands of inscrutable market forces. Bad news after a job interview. Worse news after a medical examination. The loss of loved ones. The loss of property. The loss of opportunities. The loss of love. Christians and non-Christians alike can say, 'Been there.'

As Christians we sometimes find these two sorts of suffering blended in a single circumstance. It's sorrow upon sorrow. Though we're talking about two different kinds of difficulties here, it's not like there's always a neat line that divides them in our experience. Maybe we're grieving the loss of a beloved family member, and in the midst of our grief other family members suggest we're crazy to keep holding on to the Christian faith for comfort. Suddenly we have two reasons for the same flood of tears. Or maybe one of those mocking husbands I mentioned earlier decides to bail out on the marriage because he can't stand his wife's new-found commitment to Christ, which is why she's all alone in the doctor's office the next year when she's told she has cancer. These things have happened.

A unifying principle
As soon as we acknowledge these two fundamental categories of suffering that Christians endure, an important

word of caution is in order: we need to be careful that we don't relegate the second category—that is, trials that are common in human experience—to a realm that has nothing to do with our Christian faith. That would be a serious mistake. It's true, not all of our trials are directly attributable to the fact that we are Christians, but even those that aren't, we endure *as* Christians. This is the principle that unifies all of our suffering, whatever the cause, whatever the character. This is the integrating truth that makes our life *one* life: whatever the Lord brings our way, whether unique to Christian experience or not, he calls us to face it with faith in him, and hope for heaven, and love for Christ. There may be wide variety when it comes to what we suffer and why, but *how* we handle it always has this in common: we fix our eyes on God, and we rest in his wisdom, and we seek the realization of his purposes.

In this respect, too, we're following the lead of our Saviour. We can say the same thing about Jesus: notwithstanding the variety of his sufferings, even to the end, whether distinctly messianic or commonly human, he faced it all with his eyes on his Father, resting in his wisdom, seeking his purposes. In Jesus' case, too, there may have been these various facets of experience, but they were all part of one life that he lived, guided by a single, unifying principle, which was to entrust himself to his heavenly Father in everything (1 Pet. 2:23). Once again, we aim to live like Christ as those who are in Christ. This is our living, breathing testimony to a living, sympathetic Saviour.

A most real reality

Seeking to honour Christ like this is a far better testimony than trying to tell the world—and ourselves—that pain and suffering is simply an illusion, and that we need to get in touch with reality. Sadly, some have wandered in that confused direction. The so-called 'Christian Science' of Mary Baker Eddy in the nineteenth century comes to mind. Mind over matter. But of course the real illusion is denying the reality of suffering, not the suffering itself.

Docetism was a fatal heresy about the person of Christ, claiming that his humanity was only apparent. We make the same sort of mistake when we deny, or downplay, the reality of suffering in human experience. And making that mistake only renders our faith implausible in the eyes of those who remain on the outside of it looking in. They know better. They know that any faith seems ridiculous which suggests suffering isn't real. So for the sake of witness, as well as in the interest of truth for our own souls, let us freely admit that it is real. In this way we honour Christ who truly suffered, and who even now, as man in heaven, truly remembers.

4

Suffering and Sin

In handling the truths of Scripture, we often find that we're walking a very fine line between opposite errors on our right and left. As it's sometimes put, truth is a razor's edge. Perhaps more apt than a line or edge, imagine a high wall, just wide enough for two of us to walk together side by side (though single file is safer), and we're walking along the top of that wall, making our way to a spacious landing in the distance where we'll enjoy safety again and breathe a deep sigh of relief. (I'd say, *imagine we're walking a tightrope*, but that image introduces far too much anxiety for most of us. Let's stick with the wall.) When it comes to biblical truth, errors on either side are close at hand, and we need to be careful that we don't stumble or lose our balance and fall off to one side or the other.

That axiom certainly proves true when it comes to the relationship between suffering and sin. It would be easy to get that relationship wrong in either one of two ways. Fall to the right or to the left, and great would be our fall.

Error number one

On the one hand, the first mistake we might make would be to say that there's always a direct, one-to-one, cause-and-effect connection between some form of suffering that a person experiences and some sin that they committed in the past (or are still committing in the present) for which that suffering is a chastisement from God.

This is the mistake the inhabitants of Malta make when they see Paul bitten by a poisonous viper: 'When the native people saw the creature hanging from his hand, they said to one another, "No doubt this man is a murderer. Though he has escaped from the sea, Justice has not allowed him to live"' (Acts 28:4). David Coffin has memorably referred to this as 'The Maltese Fallacy,' inspired no doubt by his love of classic films! Those islanders went wrong in that moment in a way far more fearful than any falcon.

This is also the mistake that Job's friends make in that famous Old Testament book, even as they seek to help Job make truthful sense of his trials: loss of livestock, loss of servants, loss of children, loss of health. For example, Eliphaz offers this counsel to Job: 'If iniquity is in your hand, put it far away, and let not injustice dwell in your tents. Surely then you will lift up your face without blemish; you will be secure and will not fear' (Job 11:14, 15). The implication of Eliphaz's words is that the Lord brought upon Job that terrible series of devastating losses because of some sin in Job's life, whether past or present, so that repentance would lead to restoration and blessedness instead. Later in the book, Eliphaz even gets to the point of identifying Job's sins with some specificity (see 22:4-11). And it's not just Eliphaz. Bildad and Zophar beat the same syllogistic drum: the wicked suffer; you're suffering; therefore, you must be guilty of some wickedness to which your suffering can be directly attributed. So repent already and be done with it.

No doubt those three men were earnest about God's truth, and even well-intentioned in their desire to help Job with that truth, but the fact remains that they'd gone wrong about the relationship between suffering and sin. We know this, first of all, because Job is presented to us at the beginning of the book as a 'blameless' man (1:1) whose sufferings are attributable to the extraordinary malice of Satan without any relationship to sin in Job's life (chapters 1–2). We know this, second of all, because after Eliphaz, Bildad, and Zophar have all had their say, praiseworthy Elihu steps centre-stage and contradicts those three men, even burning with anger over the false counsel that they'd offered (32:3). So in the book as a whole their cycles of speeches are bookended by material that proves them wrong.

Admittedly, there was some truth lurking in their false counsel (there usually is), and that truth needs to be acknowledged. First, the Bible does teach that sin makes for misery. Of course it does. After all, to live in opposition to the good, wise God who made us, in transgression of his prescriptions for good, wise living, is to live a life that simply doesn't work well. Try it and see: buy a tool or appliance, and promptly throw away the operator's manual written by the manufacturer, and proceed to use that item in gross violation of its purpose and design, and see what shape it's in after a year of heavy usage. (Actually, it probably won't last a year.) As Paul puts it, '[God's] law is holy, and the commandment is holy and righteous and good' (Rom. 7:12). Live against that law, and you're practically inviting frustration, or worse. Even the earthly success that people experience while living against God only masks an underlying frustration and anxiety, and their success has holes anyway. It's a hard word, but it's true: David testifies, 'Many are the sorrows of the wicked' (Psa. 32:10).

Second, sometimes there *is* an obvious, direct, one-to-one, cause-and-effect connection between some form of suffering that a person experiences and a particular sin in their life. Drive drunk, and you might spend the rest of your life in a wheelchair as a result of an automobile accident that you caused. Cheat on a test, and you might get caught, and get kicked out of school, and find that your future prospects have taken a major hit, maybe even a permanently ruinous one. Carry on an affair with another man's wife, and you might find that he finds out and finds you (Prov. 6:34).

So yes, *sometimes* there's a connection like that, and that's a possibility we ought to ponder in advance as a deterrent against sin. Sometimes God chastens his children in this way as a wise and loving Father. The mistake, however, is to go from 'sometimes' to 'always': to say that there's *always* such a connection; it's *always* the case that you can draw a straight line from transgression to trial. That's when we've fallen off our narrow wall.

Like all forms of falsehood, this one bears bitter fruit in Christians' hearts and lives, as many can attest. Lapse into this line of thinking, and you can be positively tormented when some suffering comes your way, wracking your weary brain, trying to dig up some sin-suffering connection in your past or present life, a connection that God must have buried deep and out of sight so that you'd have to work hard to find it. God's ways are turned into an inscrutable guessing game that few ever win, because few find the answer, and God himself is thus turned into a cruel kind of Father. It's no wonder Job repudiated what his three friends had to say, and that Elihu did too. Job knew it wasn't true. His conscience testified that he'd walked blamelessly before God. Job knew that their perspective was only piling sorrow upon sorrow.

Jesus knew it wasn't true as well. When his disciples asked him about a man born blind, 'Rabbi, who sinned, this man or his parents, that he was born blind?', Jesus' response was to reject their underlying assumption: 'Jesus answered, "It was not that this man sinned, or his parents, but that the works of God might be displayed in him"' (John 9:2, 3).

Paul knew it wasn't true as well. When the Lord afflicted him with what Paul refers to as 'a thorn in the flesh' (2 Cor. 12:7), it wasn't because Paul had sinned. On the contrary, as he explains to the Corinthians, it was a pre-emptive affliction to *keep* him from sinning the sin of pride going forward because the Lord had *honoured* him with an extraordinary vision of heavenly realities.

The clearest example of this principle is Christ's own experience. After all, Jesus was the man of sorrows, and he was sinless. It's certainly true that Jesus is an extraordinary figure in Scripture (to put it mildly!), with an extraordinary mission, but the very fact that he suffered in all of the ways he did (we just surveyed them in chapter 3) as a perfectly sinless man proves that God can appoint suffering in the lives of his servants that bears no direct relationship to any sin in their lives. Once again, the case of Christ is the clincher.

Error number two

If the first error was to posit a warped understanding of the relationship between suffering and sin, the error that lurks on the other side is to avoid the relationship that does in fact exist between them—perhaps out of a fear that we might be misunderstood to be guilty of Error Number One! Of course, the truth that's before us here is one that needs to be communicated with considerable pastoral sensitivity, but it *is* the truth, and we can't shrink back from it. There *is* an underlying relationship between suffering and sin, and it's this: all human suffering can finally be traced back to the human race's initial rebellion against God in the Garden of Eden.

That was the beginning.

No Fall, no suffering.

Because of the Fall, *all* suffering.

Read Genesis 3, and then Romans 5:12-21, and the Bible's teaching becomes clear: Adam, the first man, appointed by God to serve as the representative head of the human race, was put to the test—would he persevere in obedience to God?—and he failed, and his failure (really, our failure in him) led to the miseries we know now, ultimately death itself. As a result of our initial rebellion, God imposed a curse upon the human race: life on earth would now be marked by difficulty and frustration, pain and sorrow, decay and death. God told Eve that childbirth would be painful now, and that marriage would be too in its own way (Gen. 3:16), and he told Adam that the very ground he walked on and worked would oppose him now until the day he died (3:17-19), and those warnings were representative of the whole panoply of pains and problems human beings have experienced ever since. We ought to take that personally. This is no mere abstraction. All of our own pains and difficulties today, in all of their concreteness and particularity, have that same, single historical origin.

We might think that because this relationship is racial (I mean, the human race), and historical (taking us all the way back to the Fall), therefore it bears little or no practical fruit in our individual lives today. Isn't the connection too general, and too remote, to make a difference to me now? But that would be a mistake. Grasping this suffering-sin connection that goes back to the Fall has several wholesome effects in our lives.

First, it humbles us. It puts us in our place, which is on our knees before God. Sometimes when we're suffering we kid ourselves that God is in our hands, needing to explain himself to our satisfaction, when in fact we're in his.

Second, it reminds us of the truth that we *are* one human race. We fell together, as one, in Adam, our one representative, and that's why the world—this one world—is so messed up now. The notion that any particular genetic race among human beings might have standing to look down on another as fundamentally inferior, or even blame another for the problems of this world, is blasted out of the water. The Bible's teaching concerning Fall and curse is the great, dreadful equalizer.

Third, it reminds us of the justice of God. He was right to impose that curse after the Fall, which means I can raise no reasonable objection to my sufferings now. Though it needs to be said carefully, still it *can* be said about any suffering or setback I experience: 'In Adam, I deserve this. God has done me no wrong.' We can become so fearful of sounding like Job's mistaken friends ('This has happened to you because of some specific sin in your life') that we end up steering clear of this truth entirely, but to do so is to rob God of glory *he* deserves as the ever-just Judge of all the earth, and when we do that we always rob our souls of benefit too.

Fourth, it reminds us of the mercy of God. If God had dealt with the human race after the Fall according to the dictates of swift justice, then the destiny of every human being—myself included, using some Christian imagination about time and history—would have been far worse than anything I'm enduring now. As a Christian, I can always, *always* say, in any and every circumstance, that he has not dealt with me as my sin deserves.

Fifth, it reinforces for us the correlative connection between holiness and happiness. Just as God was right to impose a curse upon us after the Fall, so too will he be right to smile upon us and usher us into unimaginable blessedness at the end of the age as those who will have been made blameless in Jesus Christ in every way—as those fully justified, as those thoroughly sanctified. See? The flipside is glorious!

Finally, it points us (again) to Christ. Always a good place to be pointed, yes? We're reminded again of our merciful Saviour, the one who came into this cursed world, not deserving the curse himself, not having been represented by Adam in the Fall, and yet willingly undergoing the miseries of the curse because he had to experience to the uttermost a genuine solidarity with the people he came to save. Surely we have in him just the Saviour we need: he knew the truth of the suffering-sin connection, and (we might say) he honoured that connection by his personal descent into humanness and human suffering so as to rescue us from all our miseries. Sin won't be the final word for us. Neither will suffering. But the name of Jesus will.

5

The Lord Reigns

Whenever the topic turns to suffering, there's one particular question that looms especially large. We might phrase the question this way:

What's God got to do with it?

In other words, what are we to make of the sovereignty of God when it comes to our suffering? Is it the case that God actually brings our suffering to pass, or is his responsibility less than that? Perhaps something or someone else is the ultimate cause of what's happening to us, and God's role is limited to making wise and holy use of this development that he himself has been handed. Of course, he *is* wise and holy, so we can trust him to do so, but it would be a mistake (so goes this line of thinking) to maintain that he also brought about our pains in the first place.

For many Christians, this question becomes the proverbial elephant in the room: creating awkwardness, preferably avoided, and yet inevitably confronted. After all, this is the question that just won't go away.

The spectrum of sovereignty

Fortunately, the Bible's testimony to God's comprehensive control won't go away either. And we shouldn't want it to!

You find it, for example, in the simple refrain that seasons the Psalms: 'The Lord reigns!' (93:1; 97:1; 99:1). The people of Israel believed that their God was the royal ruler over the nations, and over their own lives, and they said so in their divinely-inspired poetry.

But it's not just in the Psalms. In the Bible it's practically everywhere! In Exodus 4:11 God says, 'Who has made man's mouth? Who makes him mute, or deaf, or seeing, or blind? Is it not I, the Lord?' In Deuteronomy 32:39 God says, 'See now that I, even I, am he, and there is no god beside me; I kill and I make alive; I wound and I heal.' In 1 Samuel 2:6, 7, Hannah says, 'The Lord kills and brings to life; he brings down to Sheol and raises up. The Lord makes poor and makes rich; he brings low and he exalts.' The list goes on: see Ecclesiastes 7:13, 14; Isaiah 45:5-7; Lamentations 3:37, 38; and Amos 3:6. Theologian Bruce Ware helpfully refers to these as 'spectrum texts' because they teach us that God's control covers the vast spectrum of things that take place in the created order: events major and minor, joyful and sorrowful, public and private, no exceptions.

Providence

The traditional theological term that Christians have used to refer to this truth of God's sovereign control is 'providence.' The Westminster Shorter Catechism defines it this way: 'God's works of providence are his most holy, wise, and powerful preserving and governing all his creatures, and all their actions' (WSC 11). Notice: it's *all* God's creatures, and all their actions too, that God preserves and governs. Notice as well that he manifests his own glory in this work: his holiness, wisdom, and power are made plain in the way he reigns—even if there are times when we mere creatures struggle to see it. (And there are.)

For a fuller statement you can always turn from the Westminster Shorter Catechism to the Westminster Confession of Faith—which isn't nearly so short!

> God the great Creator of all things doth uphold, direct, dispose, and govern all creatures, actions, and things, from the greatest even to the least, by his most wise and holy providence, according to his infallible foreknowledge, and the free and immutable counsel of his own will, to the praise of the glory of his wisdom, power, justice, goodness, and mercy. (WCF 5.1)

To be clear, in a subsequent section the Confession reminds us that God goes about this preserving and governing in a way that upholds and respects the whole system of cause-and-effect that he himself has established in the world (WCF 5.2). For example, when we say 'God provides the food we eat,' what we mean is that he rules over farmers and crops and grocery stores and grocery shopping and cooking and serving and so forth, all of which are parts of the process. And then in another section the Confession adds yet another clarification, which is that though God's providence covers even the Fall in Genesis 3 and every sin ever since, God 'neither is nor can be the author nor approver of sin' (WCF 5.4). He isn't and he can't be because he's impeccably holy. And yet this clarification is just that: it's a clarification, and not a retreat. Even the sins of human beings, beginning with the first of them in the Garden, and all of the misery that's ever resulted from them, are not beyond the parameters of providence.

The implications of this for our subject of suffering are obvious. What the Bible teaches, and therefore what God's people have long confessed, is that our God reigns sovereignly even over our pains. And he reigns not merely in the sense that he's able to bring good out of the trials that come our way (though of course that's true), but more fully in the sense that he positively brought them to pass in the first place. Go back and survey those 'spectrum texts' one more time, and notice the verbs. God is the one who kills and enlivens, who wounds and heals, who humbles and exalts. God is not merely dealt a hand that he must then play wisely. No, God is the dealer.

Though we may recognize an element of permission in God's providence—it's true to say that he upholds created things according to their natures and allows them to function according to those natures—it falls short of Scripture to say that divine permission is the whole of the story, as if it were the case that God created all things and then stepped back, out of the way, relinquishing control. No, ultimately God is the one, great, active cause of all things. He must be. He is God! This is why Paul could write to the Philippians that it had been 'granted' to them to suffer for Jesus' sake (Phil. 1:29). Granted, of course, by God himself.

Now, we hasten to add that precisely *how* God sovereignly controls the affairs of creation, including the thinking and feeling and deciding and acting of human beings, is a matter of considerable mystery to our finite and now sin-impacted minds. Of course it is. We're dealing here, after all, with the relationship between the Creator and his creation, including morally capable and responsible creatures made in his image. Of course it's the case that we're going to reach the limits of our understanding left with profound questions about the exact interplay between heaven and earth. But it's so often the case in theology—and this subject is no exception—that we may affirm *that* something is true even if we're not able for now, or ever, to understand and articulate exactly *how* it's true. And what the Bible happily forces us to conclude is that the Lord is the ultimate cause of everything I experience. No exceptions.

Christ

Here too, the example of Christ is tremendously important.

One of the clearest Bible testimonies to the truth of God's all-encompassing providence is what Scripture says about the cross.

In Acts 2, as he preached on that momentous Pentecost day, Peter said this to the people of Jerusalem who had been responsible for bringing about Jesus' death: 'this Jesus, delivered up according to the definite plan and foreknowledge of God, you crucified and killed by the hands of lawless men' (Acts 2:23). And then two chapters later Peter and his fellow apostles said it again, this time in prayer: 'for truly in this city there were gathered together against your holy servant Jesus, whom you anointed, both Herod and Pontius Pilate, along with the Gentiles and the peoples of Israel, to do whatever your hand and your plan had predestined to take place' (Acts 4:27, 28).

This testimony is clear. Here was the single greatest instance of human suffering in all of history. Remember that in his dying Jesus experienced pains far beyond those that were merely physical, and no doubt even the physical ones were agonizing in the extreme. He was bearing the very wrath of his Father in the place of his Father's people. ('But he was pierced for our transgressions; he was crushed for our iniquities'—Isa. 53:5.) The greatest suffering. Ever. And in reflecting upon it the apostles confessed in preaching and in praying that God had brought it to pass. Just as Isaiah had done so, in advance: 'Yet it was the will of the LORD to crush him; he has put him to grief' (Isa. 53:10). Indeed, the apostles confessed this even as they acknowledged the moral responsibility of the human beings who had caused the cross in their own creaturely way: Herod, Pilate, Jews, Gentiles.

And if the Father was sovereign over the pinnacle of Jesus' suffering—and the cross certainly was that—then he must have been sovereign as well over the trials and difficulties that Jesus experienced throughout his life from the beginning. All the ground we covered back in chapter 3—Jesus' sufferings both common and uncommon, from the day he was born—that was ground his Father in heaven had appointed him to tread.

And Jesus knew it. That's the key. Not only was his Father reigning over everything he experienced, but that very reality shaped the way Jesus thought about his life, and went about his ministry. It made a difference. It paid off. Consider this dramatic moment that John records for us in his Gospel account. Jesus, anticipating the sufferings of the cross, says this: 'Now is my soul troubled. And what shall I say? "Father, save me from this hour?" But for this purpose I have come to this hour. Father, glorify your name' (John 12:27, 28). Jesus naturally recoiled from the prospect of the pains that were in store for him. As true man, he couldn't *not* react that way. And yet he knew that it was his Father's sovereign purpose that he finally experience those pains, and that he do so for the redemption of his people. And it was that truth that kept him going, down into depths that no one else ever experienced before or since.

We get another glimpse of this the night before he died. In the Garden of Gethsemane, Jesus went off by himself, and he prayed that famous prayer: 'My Father, if it be possible, let this cup pass from me; nevertheless, not as I will, but as you will' (Matt. 26:39). And then he prayed it again. And then he prayed it again. And what was the result? Jesus came away from those moments of fellowship with his Father only reinforced in the conviction that his Father had indeed appointed great suffering as his calling. So once again, determined to heed the call, Jesus kept going. And because he did so, there is salvation for our souls.

In this respect we Christians are called to follow the lead of the Christ. Obviously none of us is called like Christ to suffer and die to save sinners. But we are called to make our way through a world of tears in which we shed our own because of griefs and trials that come our way. And just like Jesus, we can rest in the thought that it's our wise and loving Father in heaven who has appointed them for us. And just as it did for Jesus, that truth can bear the sweet fruits of consolation, and determination, and hopefulness for the day when crosses will finally give way to joys (Heb. 12:2).

Conclusion

I said at the outset of this chapter that the relationship between God's sovereignty and our suffering can be the elephant in the room, the topic we don't want to touch. Since elephants sometimes strike us as relatively benign creatures (though they're not; see YouTube), perhaps we should call it the *lion* in the room instead. Some Christians do find this truth to be rather frightening to confront, especially when they see that it's charging right for them!

But once again the call of the gospel is, 'Fear not.' Yes, the truth of God's sovereignty over our suffering can be a challenging one to contemplate, perhaps even unnerving at first. And yes, it does charge at us from the pages of Scripture, swift and agile and relentless. A leonine truth, indeed! But Christian, fear not. This lion charges and pounces not to devour, but to rescue. When you realize that the lion is for you and not against you, how glad you become when you hear him roar.

6

Forged by Affliction

The truth we considered in the previous chapter—God is the ultimate sovereign source even of our suffering in this life—leads us directly into our next theme, which is his purposes for bringing Christians' trials to pass. How important it is that we know those purposes! Apart from the conviction that God intends to do us good by our suffering, we would be left uncertain—or worse, terrified—by the thought of comprehensive divine providence. Remember that lion at the end of the last chapter? We *would* be terrified if we had reason to believe he meant to devour us, or if we simply suspected that this might be the case. So it is with God.

If all we have to believe in is the bare thought that there's a supreme being who holds our lives in his hands, a being who's perfectly willing to inflict pain upon us, and we're left in the dark about what he's like and how he feels about us and what he finally intends to do with us, then that bare thought becomes a frightening one. We're left with the possibility that this supreme being is a tyrant or a sadist whose treatment of us will prove it. Thankfully, we're given a whole lot more in Scripture than just the notion of bare sovereignty! The Bible tells us what God is like, and how deeply he loves his children, and what his loving purposes are whenever he does put them through pain.

In this chapter and in the two that follow, our aim will be to explore those purposes and to glean from them the instruction and encouragement they contain. We can't cover God's purposes exhaustively, of course. That would transform this 'mini-guide' into something most un-mini! But we'll seek to survey some leading biblical themes.

Why?

To consider the Bible's teaching about God's purposes for our suffering is to face The Big Question that many wrestle with in times of trial. That question is—'*Why? Why am I suffering like this?*' It's true that some ask that question while shaking a clenched, bitter fist at heaven. In the midst of their pains, they sinfully demand that God take his place in the defendant's seat and give an account of his actions, and they do so already having determined to find his account inadequate and to pronounce him guilty of malpractice.

But the question doesn't have to be asked like that. A genuine believer might humbly, worshipfully wonder about the purposes of the God he loves, and crave whatever light Scripture has to shed. In that case 'Why?' is a very different question, and a God-honouring one.

Remember that high, narrow wall at the beginning of chapter 4? The narrow wall of truth that we tread with errors on either side? Well, whenever we ask the question 'Why does God cause his people to suffer?' we're walking such a narrow path once again. On the one hand, we want to make the most of what Scripture does teach us about the purposes of God for our trials. As we'll see over these next few chapters, God has not been silent on this subject. God has spoken. God has told us much about what he's up to and why.

On the other hand, we need to be careful that we don't expect from Scripture more than Scripture can possibly provide. Sometimes we want to know precisely how this or that circumstance we're enduring is contributing to the advancement of God's cause in the world, and in our own lives, but to expect that from the Bible is to expect too much. Not because the Bible is insufficient, but simply because the Bible isn't that kind of book. Indeed, it *can't* be that kind of book! In the nature of the case the Bible has to be a revelation from God that gives us general principles about his ways of working. So we need to avoid both errors: (1) expecting answers to every single detailed question we might ask, or (2) lapsing into total agnosticism as if there were no answers at all.

Character

One of the answers the Bible gives to this question is that God brings about our suffering for the purpose of changing us, so that we grow in holiness. 'Sanctification,' says the Westminster Shorter Catechism, 'is the work of God's free grace, whereby we are renewed in the whole man after the image of God, and are enabled more and more to die unto sin, and live unto righteousness' (WSC 35). And the Bible teaches us that God tests and tries us as a way of accomplishing that gracious, transforming, lifelong work.

Consider, for example, the testimony of the author of Psalm 119. That psalm is the longest in the Psalter, celebrating the word of God in a wide variety of ways, and close to the middle of it we find this pair of verses:

> Before I was afflicted I went astray, but now I keep your word (verse 67).

> It is good for me that I was afflicted, that I might learn your statutes (verse 71).

This psalmist who so loved the word of God also recognized that God had brought about affliction in his life for the express purpose of driving him to that word. It could be that his affliction was the direct result of his having departed from God's word in some way, so that his trials had the effect of bringing him back to the path he never should have left. But that isn't necessarily the case. It could be that his affliction wasn't the direct result of sin at all, but it still drove him to the word as the source of truth he desperately needed to steady and guide and encourage him through his pains. Whatever the precise circumstance may have been, he could actually say that it was good for him to be afflicted.

Of course, this doesn't mean the affliction was to be celebrated *because* it caused pain. This is a misunderstanding of Christianity, and in some cases a deliberate distortion and caricature: the idea that Christians relish the thought of feeling pain and even seek it out as that which curries favour with God. No, the psalmist's affliction was good, not because of its intrinsic painfulness, but because of how God was using it to teach and transform him. This is why the believer can acknowledge the spiritual usefulness of his afflictions in this world, at the same time that he longs for the world to come in which afflictions will be no more.

Moving from Old Testament to New, the letters of the apostles reinforce and develop this same idea, that God uses our suffering to sanctify us. See how Paul puts it in Romans 5: 'we rejoice in our sufferings, knowing that suffering produces endurance, and endurance produces character, and character produces hope, and hope does not put us to shame, because God's love has been poured into our hearts through the Holy Spirit who has been given to us' (Rom. 5:3-5). This is a beautiful chain of Christian virtues—endurance, character, hope—and Paul is putting it plainly that God uses our sufferings to produce those virtues.

When we suffer, we learn valuable lessons about what it means to keep going as Christians come what may, and we grow in that very capacity (endurance). And as we endure through sufferings we're forged in a well-rounded way, becoming men and women of steady fidelity and integrity (character). And as we develop and demonstrate that character we grow in our hopefulness for heaven, because it's a heavenly holiness that's increasingly on display in our lives. And if God has begun to make us heavenly now, then he won't fail to get us there in the end (Phil. 1:6). This is why Paul can say to the Corinthians that 'this light momentary affliction is preparing for us an eternal weight of glory beyond all comparison' (2 Cor. 4:17). Our affliction in this life is preparing eternal glory for us because God is using it to forge in our lives the character of the world to come. And that's exactly why Paul can describe our present affliction as 'light and momentary' in comparison.

The apostle James sounds a similar note in the opening verses of his letter. 'Count it all joy, my brothers, when you meet trials of various kinds, for you know that the testing of your faith produces steadfastness. And let steadfastness have its full effect, that you may be perfect and complete, lacking in nothing' (James 1:2-4). As the writer of Hebrews puts it, our heavenly Father 'disciplines us for our good, that we may share his holiness. For the moment all discipline seems painful rather than pleasant, but later it yields the peaceful fruit of righteousness to those who have been trained by it' (Heb. 12:10, 11).

Christ

It might seem strange—or worse, positively blasphemous—to connect even this truth with the experience of Christ. After all, Jesus was perfectly sinless, and therefore he didn't need to be transformed by suffering as we do from sinner to saint. Surely we've wandered into questionable theological territory to suggest that there's some link here between Christ's experience and our own.

But upon closer biblical examination, it isn't so strange, and it certainly isn't blasphemous. Yes, we do affirm that Jesus lived the whole of his life without sin (Heb. 4:15). And so we do affirm that Jesus didn't need to be sanctified exactly as we do, including the mortification of sin. And yet it is the Bible's teaching that sinless Jesus, by virtue of his true humanity, did grow in his experience of love for God. Luke says so: 'Jesus increased in wisdom and in stature and in favour with God and man' (Luke 2:52).

There was no sin in Jesus that had to be put to death, and yet it is the nature of human experience, even apart from sin, that our understanding of what it means to love God grows with time and testing, and this love increasingly fills our lives with the development of our natural capacities for knowing and feeling and willing.

And the Bible further teaches that Jesus experienced this growth because of the suffering his Father brought him through: 'Although he was a son, he learned obedience through what he suffered' (Heb. 5:8). Again, no mortification of sin in Jesus' case. But learning and growing all the same.

Revisiting those two verses from Psalm 119, we can put it this way. Jesus could never say, 'Before I was afflicted I went astray, but now I keep your word' (verse 67). After all, Jesus never went astray. But he certainly *could* say, 'It is good for me that I was afflicted, that I might learn your statutes' (verse 71). There was no folly in Jesus' life that had to be undone, but there certainly was learning that took place, even learning the statutes of his Father's word, as he studied and applied those statutes as a boy, and then as a man, and then as a teacher-healer under fire.

Conclusion

So it turns out there *is* a link, and a tremendously valuable one, between Christ's experience and our own. If the sinless, incarnate Son of God had to experience suffering in order to learn experientially what it means to love God, and to grow in that love in a truly human way, then should we be surprised to find that God appoints suffering in our lives too, in order to make us more like Christ? Never forget, 'a servant is not greater than his master' (John 13:16). How wonderful it is to be his servants, and to be able to fix our gaze on the Master as we suffer and weep and hope, and thus follow in Jesus' truly human steps.

7

The Compassion of the Comforted

In our previous chapters we've seen that God is the one who brings trials our way, and that he does so in order to change us, causing us even to share in his holiness.

One aspect of that holy divine character that's forged in us is his compassion for the downtrodden. Our God draws near to his people in their broken-heartedness. David says so in Psalm 34: 'When the righteous cry for help, the LORD hears and delivers them out of all their troubles. The LORD is near to the brokenhearted and saves the crushed in spirit' (Psa. 34:17, 18).

The word 'brokenhearted' is a common expression, familiar to our ears, so it doesn't throw us to read it. But the parallel descriptor 'crushed in spirit' isn't so common, and for that very reason it's especially potent. It gets our attention. Haven't we all felt that way at times? So heavily burdened by some sorrow, so thoroughly devastated by some loss, that it feels like we've been positively crushed deep within. Well, God saves people who have been laid low like that. He visits them by his word and Spirit, reassuring them with the truth of his gospel, and thus giving their spirits shape and strength and wholeness again.

We read the same thing in Psalm 147: 'He heals the brokenhearted and binds up their wounds' (Psa. 147:3). This is especially remarkable because the very next verse says, 'He determines the number of the stars; he gives to all of them their names' (verse 4). Staggering! The same God who created and arranged the very hosts of heaven with almighty power and unsearchable wisdom also draws near to weeping men and women in beautiful tenderness, wrapping them in a loving embrace, consoling them with the thought of his love, wiping away their tears, and enabling them to rise up and carry on and hope for heaven. This is our God!

And this is also an aspect of what it means that our suffering makes us like God. The temptation we face in times of trial is to become self-absorbed, practically forgetting that any other human being exists, and having an eye toward no other outcome than the cessation of our own pain and the experience of relief. But God's purpose for our suffering is to make us loving as he is loving, and to give us opportunities to show it. God intends to mould and shape us into people who derive deep comfort from his word as we travel into trials, and who then bless others with that same comfort as we find them travelling there too. In short, he makes us into people who open our eyes, and our hearts. With eyes wide open, we read our Bibles in the midst of our difficulties, perhaps with tears in those eyes, finding there the gospel we need in order to press on. And then keeping our eyes open, we look up and look around and notice that other human beings *do* in fact exist, and that they're hurting too, and with open hearts we seize opportunities to show them the comforts that we've known. This is what it means for us as redeemed creatures to mirror the character of our kind and loving Creator-Redeemer. We come across brothers and sisters in Christ who are crushed in spirit, and we come alongside them to be the agents of God's consoling, healing work in their lives, just as others have been in ours before and continue to be.

2 Corinthians 1

This comes through crystal clear in what Paul says at the beginning of 2 Corinthians:

> Blessed be the God and Father of our Lord Jesus Christ, the Father of mercies and God of all comfort, who comforts us in all our affliction, so that we may be able to comfort those who are in any affliction, with the comfort with which we ourselves are comforted by God. For as we share abundantly in Christ's sufferings, so through Christ we share abundantly in comfort too. If we are afflicted, it is for your comfort and salvation; and if we are comforted, it is for your comfort, which you experience when you patiently endure the same sufferings that we suffer. Our hope for you is unshaken, for we know that as you share in our sufferings, you will also share in our comfort (2 Cor. 1:3-7).

What a remarkable passage. If we didn't know better we might think Paul wrote that passage on a dare to see how many times he could use words meaning 'comfort' in the course of five verses! (It's ten times, by the way. Mixed with six instances of words meaning 'affliction' or 'suffering.' This is decidedly *not* one of those passages that leaves you wondering what its main theme is.)

Consider the pattern Paul describes here.

First, he and his fellow workers in ministry suffered in the course of that ministry. And suffered dearly. If you'd like to learn more about the particulars of those sufferings, skip down to 2 Corinthians 11:23—and fasten your seatbelt. Because in that passage Paul takes us on quite a tour of the hardships he'd known. Labours. Imprisonments. Beatings. And that's just the first verse. And notice (back now to our passage in chapter 1), this was to 'share abundantly in Christ's sufferings.' That is, they were experiencing in their own bodies what it meant to live and serve in union with the one who'd suffered to the uttermost, and who warned his servants that they could expect a measure of the same (John 15:18-20).

Next, Paul and those with him had known comforts from God in the midst of that suffering. Paul doesn't unpack here in chapter 1 what those comforts were, but it's not hard for us to fill in that blank. For that matter, the rest of 2 Corinthians fills in the blank for us. They'd have been comforted, for example, by the truth that God 'in Christ always leads us in triumphal procession, and through us spreads the fragrance of the knowledge of him everywhere' (2:14). And by the good news that 'we all, with unveiled face, beholding the glory of the Lord, are being transformed into the same image from one degree of glory to another' (3:18). And by the truth that 'God, who said, "Let light shine out of darkness," has shone in our hearts to give the light of the knowledge of the glory of God in the face of Jesus Christ' (4:6). And by the message that 'for our sake [God] made him to be sin who knew no sin, so that in him we might become the righteousness of God' (5:21). (We could keep going throughout the letter, but you get the idea.) In 2 Corinthians it's one sweet gospel truth after another. Paul and those serving with him clung to those truths in the midst of their labours and imprisonments and beatings and all the rest. That's why he could say, 'We are afflicted in every way, but not crushed; perplexed, but not driven to despair; persecuted, but not forsaken; struck down, but not destroyed' (4:8, 9).

Finally, Paul and his fellow-workers were able to pass on to the Corinthians the comforts that they themselves had experienced first. That's what completed the pattern. Indeed, as we just noticed, 2 Corinthians itself, chock-full of reassuring truths in chapter after chapter, was one of the means of their doing so. The Lord was near to Paul in his broken-heartedness, so that Paul might then be near to others who were suffering too.

It's certainly true that in this 2 Corinthians 1 passage Paul is reflecting upon his own experience as an apostle, but it's safe to say that this threefold pattern is the shape of common Christian experience. Believers suffer in union with their Saviour, and that's when God draws near with the gospel, and that's what enables them to turn around and tell fellow Christian sufferers that the pain won't prevail, and to show kindness to all in his name.

Christ

Here too, we can cast our gaze upon Christ and see this truth so beautifully displayed.

Remember the verses in Hebrews 5 that we've noticed before:

> In the days of his flesh, Jesus offered up prayers and supplications, with loud cries and tears, to him who was able to save him from death, and he was heard because of his reverence. Although he was a son, he learned obedience through what he suffered. And being made perfect, he became the source of eternal salvation to all who obey him (Heb. 5:7-9).

What we learn there is that Jesus himself, pained as he was, truly suffering in his true humanity, had to cry out to his Father in heaven for comfort. And naturally he got it. His Father did comfort him. Jesus loved his Father's word, and he would have been able to glean from that word in close fellowship with his Father the truths and promises that held him up and drove him forward. And to what end? For what purpose? For the purpose that he might be forged by that experience so as to become the Saviour his people need him to be, one who is able to save the crushed in spirit, able to heal the brokenhearted and bind up their wounds. Jesus 'endured the cross' with his eyes fixed on 'the joy that was set before him' (Heb. 12:2), and now he is able to comfort cross-carrying Christians with the thought that joy awaits them too in eternal heavenly fellowship with himself, so that they can endure like he did. In short, he suffered so as to sympathize.

The writer of Hebrews says so explicitly in the previous chapter: 'For we do not have a high priest who is unable to sympathize with our weaknesses, but one who in every respect has been tempted as we are, yet without sin' (Heb. 4:15). Jesus knows. Jesus understands. Jesus sympathizes. He himself was comforted by God in the midst of his own loud cries and tears, and now from heaven he comforts us by word and Spirit with the comfort with which he himself was comforted by God, which is the truth of the gospel.

This is why it can be said that it's 'better' (a word that's all over Hebrews) to know God now, after the coming of Christ, compared to knowing him in Old Testament times. It's true, as we've already seen, David could testify in his own time, 'The Lord is near to the brokenhearted and saves the crushed in spirit' (Psa. 34:18). God dealt compassionately with his people Israel, and they knew it, and they said so.

But now in Jesus Christ God has drawn near to his people in a new way: in the fullness of time he sent his own Son to become flesh and dwell among us—and suffer among us too. And now the incarnate Son, whose sufferings have been completed but who has not forgotten, is seated at the Father's right hand in heaven as a faithful friend for Christians who suffer still on earth. The compassion of

God is mediated to us now by the God-man Christ Jesus. A Saviour who can say to his suffering people, 'I understand! I've been there!' A Saviour who can pour into their lives the very comforts he once received, and who does so by the same Spirit who comforted him. This reality lends a new dimension of solidarity and sympathy to our knowledge and experience of God's compassion. Better, indeed!

Conclusion

Let's learn this lesson well. This is one of the purposes of God for our suffering. That we should follow Jesus' lead, blessing others with the comforts that our sufferings have made sweet to our own souls. So let's open our eyes, and open our hearts, entering into our Bibles, and then entering into the lives of our brothers and sisters in Jesus around us. Christ is able to sympathize. In union with him, we are too. Let's show ourselves to be the people of the 'God of all comfort.' In this way our suffering will not have been in vain.

8

Suffering and Witness

Our consideration of God's purposes for our suffering has been moving outward in concentric circles in these chapters. We started with God's purpose with respect to our own character: his aim is to make us holy. That's the one that hits closest to home, and deep within. Then we moved outward to consider how our suffering equips us to comfort brothers and sisters in Christ who are enduring trials of their own. In this chapter we'll take one more outward step. Here our theme is the usefulness of our suffering to strengthen the church's witness in the world, and thus advance the spread of the gospel.

Acts

The book that follows the four Gospel accounts in our Bibles has been given the traditional name 'Acts,' because it recounts for us the actions of the apostles after the ascension of Jesus into heaven. We can imagine an alternative title. How about calling it 'Sufferings'?! Practically from the beginning, the book we call 'Acts' is a relentless chronicle of the things that Jesus' people (including the apostles) had to suffer for the sake of making him known. What Jesus says about Paul at the time of his conversion and call to ministry serves as a banner that hangs over the whole book, covering Peter and the other apostles as well, and then the church as a whole: 'I will show him how much he must suffer for the sake of my name' (Acts 9:16).

What also stands out as we make our way through the book is how regularly the Lord uses the suffering of his servants to spread the gospel and bring people to faith. When Jesus said to his disciples prior to his ascension, 'you will be my witnesses in Jerusalem and in all Judea and Samaria, and to the end of the earth' (1:8), he might have added, 'and your witness will be blood-stained. Every step of the way.'

Consider, for example, the tremendous advance of the gospel among the Jews in Jerusalem that we read about in the early chapters. That advance takes place, in part because of the remarkable testimony of the first Christians in that city, and what made their testimony so remarkable was their willingness to suffer for the message they were proclaiming. Indeed, they weren't just willing to suffer for Christ; they were actually found 'rejoicing that they were counted worthy to suffer dishonour for the name' (after being beaten, 5:41). No wonder 'the people held them in high esteem' (that is, unbelieving people, 5:13). And no wonder the Lord used their testimony to bring thousands to Christ. Their words about Jesus came with extraordinary weight and power because they were seasoned with such evident commitment and courage.

The persecution of the church in Jerusalem reaches a climax in the trial and stoning of faithful Stephen, which we read about in chapters 6 and 7. When Stephen stands before the Jewish ruling council and charges them with murdering Jesus like the murder of prophets in the Old Testament, his words are too much for them to take, and they stone him to death (7:58-60). We can only imagine the impression that this dreadful, wonderful episode made on that young man Saul, later to be known as Paul, who approved of Stephen's execution (8:1). Luke doesn't tell us. But it isn't hard to imagine that Stephen's willingness to suffer and die for Jesus stayed with Paul, and in time was used by the Lord as a means of encouraging Paul in his own similar service. How poignant that Paul should later follow the example of a man whose unjust execution he himself sanctioned and witnessed.

Then, after Stephen's martyrdom, the persecution that erupted in Jerusalem led to the spread of the gospel beyond that city: 'And there arose on that day a great persecution against the church in Jerusalem, and they were all scattered throughout the regions of Judea and Samaria, except the apostles' (8:1). At this point Saul is still the Anti-Christ Ravager, and not yet the Christian Preacher, but the Lord is using Saul's hateful efforts as a means of driving Christians into the surrounding regions and sending the gospel with them.

This same principle finally plays out in the life of Paul himself. It's Paul, like no one else, who will be the Lord's instrument to take the gospel to the ends of the earth (9:15), and his pains and persecutions will sharpen him as such an instrument. Just as Jesus was made a perfect Saviour by virtue of his suffering and what he learned from it (Heb. 5:8, 9), so Paul was to be made a complete apostle in the same way.

Here's just one example. In Acts 16, when Paul and Silas go to the great city of Philippi and preach the gospel, their reward from the city authorities is to be beaten and jailed in violation of Roman law. This is wickedness! This is injustice! This is persecution! So this is—*time to sing*?

Apparently so. Luke describes the late night jail scene: 'About midnight Paul and Silas were praying and singing hymns to God, and the prisoners were listening to them' (16:25). The groans of suffering are being drowned out by the melodies of praise. And then that singing time turns into salvation time for one man and his family: the jailer himself, of all people. In the chaos right after an earthquake that strikes the site, the jailer asks Paul and Silas, '"Sirs, what must I do to be saved?" And they said, "Believe in the Lord Jesus, and you will be saved, you and your household"' (16:30, 31).

Epilogue: he did, and they were. The cruel pains to which Paul and Silas were subjected led straight to this man's salvation, and to the incorporation of his whole household within the orbit of God's grace, and no doubt to the furthering of the gospel cause in Philippi more broadly. (Especially when the city authorities had to admit after the fact—and publicly—that they'd been wrong to treat Paul and Silas as they did.)

It's also worth underlining (stepping aside now from Acts) that Paul was perfectly willing, even determined, to make mention of his sufferings in the letters he wrote. It's not just the litany of hardships we've noticed in 2 Corinthians 11. It's also Galatians 6:17: 'I bear on my body the marks of Jesus.' (See also 1 Thessalonians 2:2 and 2 Timothy 3:11.) And why? Why should Paul so regularly and so freely remind people of his suffering? Was he full of self-pity? Was he self-absorbed? Far from it. Paul was *Christ*-absorbed, and Paul knew that the cause of Christ's gospel would be strengthened if it were known far and wide that Christ's pre-eminent servant had suffered for that cause. Especially since Paul was often charged with being a charlatan! Paul's reputation had evangelistic significance, and he knew it.

Paul knew that if he had a reputation for being a fraud, then his message would likely be seen as fraudulent too, and then that becomes just one more excuse for people not to believe it. Put positively, Paul knew that his own willingness to suffer for Christ (like Stephen's before him) could silence slanderers and reinforce his appeal that sinners be reconciled to God. It wasn't self-pity. It was pity for those who remained cut off from Christ, and who needed to know that this messenger of Christ bore on his body the marks of sincerity and truth. 'Charlatan' was the charge. 'I've suffered for this' was an important part of the answer.

Today

Though much has changed since those first-century days, still the principle remains in place: one of God's purposes for the suffering of his people is that the message of the gospel should go forth with particular forcefulness, rescuing the lost, changing lives, creating churches, creating hope.

Consider how this principle continues to manifest itself. Even today, there are missionaries and church-planters who leave home to labour in a particular community, only to discover that opposition or indifference to the gospel in that place makes it wise for them to change their plans and move elsewhere. But then they find in their new location that the Lord has opened hearts there, and that they're perfectly positioned to reap the harvest. Or maybe that missionary concludes that remaining where opposition is brewing is the best course, and that becomes the setting where their faith shines, and in that light others see the light, and enter in. So too, there are Christians today who can look back and see how the Lord brought them to faith, in part by means of the testimony of other Christians who sacrificially stood their ground for the gospel. Those other believers bore the marks of Jesus on their bodies, or on their earthly fortunes, and that made their gospel too much for that person to resist.

Sometimes the connection is less direct than those instances. For example, we've seen that God uses suffering to make his people more like Christ, including more compassionate. The evidence of that very Christlikeness, forged in trial, and then displayed in daily living and in the fellowship of the church, is often used by the Lord to lead others to himself. It has the effect of lending power to the church's pleas.

This is particularly striking when, as sometimes takes place, the one who's weighing the claims of Christ is himself suffering in some fashion. The Lord works that way too. He uses some sudden devastating loss, or some unrelenting lifelong pressure, to drive a person to his knees where he's forced to consider Christ in a new way, perhaps even for the first time. When that person looks at the people of Christ and finds that they understand suffering too, and that they're still believing and walking with Christ in the midst of their own pains, that shows him that this Jesus really is the Saviour of the crushed in spirit, and that the brokenhearted don't have to find a way to wipe their tears away before they believe. If they can look at the church and see that God's people are making their way to God's kingdom through many tribulations (Acts 14:22), it makes the church's gospel ring true.

To this day the church's ongoing book of 'Sufferings' is being written. The gospel is going forward into communities, into souls, and in a host of ways the Lord is using the testing and trials of his people to get it there.

Christ

We shouldn't be surprised by this. After all, at the heart of the Christian message is the claim that God's Son suffered and died to save. That truth touches down here in these two ways.

First, the work of Christ to save sinners from death *by* death tells us that God is able and willing to use suffering to bring about gracious and glorious outcomes. God uses that which is awful and dark to produce that which is beautiful and brilliant. So it was with the work of Christ; so it is now for the people of Christ. The missionary, for example, who finds that his suffering in one place leads to the salvation of others in another place can say, 'Of course! The cross could have taught me that.' The cross, which gave way to the empty tomb, teaches us that suffering brings about glory. God works that way. He did so in Christ's death-and-resurrection mission, and he does so now in the church's preaching-and-praying mission too.

Second, since Jesus suffered and told his people to expect suffering in his steps, and since the church now proclaims this about him, their faith and faithfulness during trials have the effect of reinforcing and vindicating their argument. Put simply, it fits the message. There's a match. Put negatively, there's a terrible *mis*-match when Christians talk about a suffering Saviour but then live as those obsessed with maximizing comfort and avoiding pain, even side-stepping aspects of Christian truth in order to do so. Of course, unbelief is never excusable, never justifiable, but this kind of mismatch between Christians' words and lives does make the gospel appear less plausible in the world's eyes, and therefore robs it of some of the practical power it ought to possess. Far better that our lives should 'adorn the doctrine of God our Saviour' (Titus 2:10). The gospel doesn't need us to make it true and beautiful, but a watching world does need us to live in such a way as to show it. So may we live!

Conclusion

There are so many reasons Christians are drawn to the book of Acts. I still remember my first read-through as a new believer. I could hardly put it down, and didn't want it to end! The history is dramatic, the stories gripping, the major and minor characters compelling. No wonder the book draws us in. And this is part of it: we find in Acts the gospel advancing in and through the testing of those first Christians, who are our brothers and sisters from long ago. They suffered, and because they did so 'the word of God increased and multiplied' (Acts 12:24). That's a good and vital word for us today. God remains the same, and so do his purposes and his manner of fulfilling them.

9

FAQs: Satan's Role, and God's Control

On the subject of suffering, there are quite a few 'Frequently Asked Questions' that people pose. In this chapter and the two that follow, we'll address several of them, and seek to shed more clarifying light on what the Bible does and does not teach on this subject.

Like most FAQ sections on websites, these chapters will roam a bit and cover a variety of separate topics. This is analogous to those sections in the book of Deuteronomy given the heading 'Miscellaneous Laws' in our Bibles. Separate, and miscellaneous, but still vital!

Satan's role

Remember, the question we asked and answered way back in chapter 5 was, when it comes to suffering, what's God got to do with it? (Is he truly sovereign over it? Answer: yes.) Here the question sounds similar: what's *Satan* got to do with it? Is the devil involved in human suffering?

Does he positively bring it to pass? Some of it? All of it? Or does he just pile on when it's already happening and try to intensify it? Or does he simply seek to take advantage of it for some nefarious spiritual purpose? Or is it all of the above—and more?!

This question is inspired in part by Satan's doings in the book of Job. That book is the first one that comes to many people's minds when they think about suffering in Scripture—it's a classic and much-studied tale—and it's well known that Satan plays a key part right at the outset. (Well known to the reader, that is, though not to Job.) At first the Lord permits Satan to strike devastating blows against Job's family and fortunes, and then when that doesn't work (at least from Satan's perspective, because Job doesn't curse God), the Lord allows Satan to strike Job personally. Which he does. Fiercely. By the end of chapter 2, Satan has laid Job very, very low, and the rest of the book is a coming to grips with Job's trials.

Beyond the book of Job, we get some other glimpses. Consider Satan's role in bringing about the sufferings of Christ: Satan led Judas to betray Jesus (Luke 22:3), which led to Jesus' arrest and all that followed. Consider also Paul's rather matter-of-fact mention of Satan as the one who had thwarted Paul's plans to visit and encourage the Thessalonians (1 Thess. 2:18). Clearly this is a creature whom God permits to exercise his power in a way that touches human lives, and his power to cause pain is considerable. Naturally all of this leaves us wondering, what can we conclude about Satan's involvement in human suffering generally?

Proceed with caution

Like many (perhaps all!) questions in theology, this one has us walking that narrow wall again, with the danger of falling off into errors on either side. Let's proceed with caution. On the one hand, we need to acknowledge the evidence we've marshalled here. The implication is clear that Satan is directly involved, at least on occasion, with God's permission, in the sufferings that human beings experience (including profound losses and sorrows, like Job's). And it's also true that Satan seeks in unseen deceitful ways to capitalize on our sufferings by using them to lead us away from God. That's always his goal.

He is, as Jesus said, a murderer and liar (John 8:44). He is, as Paul said, a deceiver who 'disguises himself as an angel of light' (2 Cor. 11:14). He is, as Peter said, an 'adversary [who] prowls around like a roaring lion, seeking someone to devour,' so that Christians need to watch and resist (1 Pet. 5:8). And let's not forget what we saw back in chapter 4: all human suffering can be traced back to our Fall in Genesis 3, which Satan set in motion. Put all of these pieces together and a fearful biblical portrait comes into view. As Paul puts it, 'we are not ignorant of his designs' (2 Cor. 2:11).

On the other hand—and this is vitally important—we also need to acknowledge the limits of what Scripture shows us, and of what we're able to perceive in our own day-to-day experience. Yes, we can say as a general truth that sometimes God allows Satan to act directly in human affairs, but we have no way of knowing the precise part, if any, Satan has played in some specific suffering that's happening to us, and in how that circumstance is affecting us. And the good news (though I realize it sounds strange to call any of this news 'good') is that we don't need to know that. It's wasted energy for me to go around wondering if the devil has done this or that to me. Instead I should pour myself into what Scripture *does* reveal, and to the good fight Scripture calls me to wage. It's enough to know that Satan is real, and that his malice is awful, and that he's at work, and that lies are his stock-in-trade, and that Christ is far greater, and that we're called to fix our eyes on Jesus as the one who guides us in truth and gives us the victory. Remember, Christian, 'he who is in you is greater than he who is in the world' (1 John 4:4).

We might think it's useless to know that Satan is active if I can't know exactly *how* he's been involved in a given situation. But it's not useless at all. That knowledge drives me to Christ with renewed trust, and gets me opening my Bible with renewed humility, and stirs me to long for Satan's judgment on the last day. Faith, and truth, and hope. These and other graces make up the panoply of God with which we're to be armed (Eph. 6:10-20). And all of that is perfectly possible and eminently practical even though the curtain isn't pulled back in my life (as it is sometimes in Scripture) so that I can see precisely what the devil is up to in a particular circumstance. Our calling is a biblical blending of trembling and trusting—without paralyzing ourselves by peering into things that remain hidden (Deut. 29:29).

Satan's cause

Never forget: Satan's fundamental disposition isn't that of chief pain-maker. Instead, he's creation's arch rebel. That is, a rebel against God. Therefore his cause in our lives isn't just to hurt us. It's to make us rebels too. It's to lead us away from God, and thus make us more like himself. C. S. Lewis's imaginary demon Screwtape had to remind his nephew Wormwood of this point, lest the latter get overly excited about an earthly war breaking out, with its concomitant earthly trials: 'Of course a war is entertaining. The immediate fear and suffering of the humans is a legitimate and pleasing refreshment for our myriads of toiling workers. But what permanent good does it do us unless we make use of it for bringing souls to our father Below?'[1]

Whenever reading *The Screwtape Letters* we should take Screwtape's wicked counsel and flip it: Christian, fix your eyes on God. Whatever Satan's precise part may be in bringing your pains to pass, the way to frustrate his purposes is by running to God instead of drifting away from him. And don't be afraid to name your enemy in prayer now and then. Doing so can make all this seem more real. 'Father, Satan wants this suffering to drive me away from you. By your grace it won't happen. Here I stand. God help me.'

And he will.

God's control

A natural follow-up question at this point is a variation on the inevitable and heartfelt 'Why?' that we've posed before.

[1] C. S. Lewis, *The Screwtape Letters*, ch. 5.

In previous chapters we canvassed God's holy purposes for our trials, and that's vital biblical truth, but the question remains: could God not have accomplished his purposes (namely, his glory and our good) in a different way? Why did it have to be *this* way? Why did it have to be *this* kind of world in the first place? Without any difficulty, God could have struck Satan down in his rebellion prior to his tempting Eve, and brought it to pass that the Fall and human suffering never happened. So why didn't he? What a different world it might have been. No sin and misery, ever. Even if we allow for the Fall and suffering, we're still left asking, 'God, did it have to be this bad? Couldn't you have realized your aims with a minimum of human pain?'

These are no mere ivory-tower speculations. These questions come practically howling out of our souls when we're confronted with domestic violence, and teen suicide, and mass shootings, and war crimes, and refugee crises. This awful world we're living in—a world in which wives are beaten and young people are driven to end it all and movie-goers are gunned down and hospitals are shelled and children are forced to flee for their lives—is this the world that had to be?

Just to pose these questions is to be driven to our knees. Once again, we're brought face-to-face with the reality of our own finitude. We're not in the position to peer beyond this universe into the ones that might have been, or to parse out God's reasons for all that happens. The most we can say is that God is good, and that therefore he must have his own good rationale for the whole plan he's brought to pass, and that he calls us to trust in him even when things don't make sense and we don't have answers. I vividly recall a seminary classroom Q&A session in the immediate aftermath of the shooting at Columbine High School in Littleton, Colorado on 20 April 1999. The professor was asked, 'If you found yourself in the company of parents whose children were killed that day, and one of those parents asked you, "Why? Why did this happen?", what would you say?' He paused, and then replied, and his thoughtful reply included words to this effect:

> God's word enables me, and even calls me, to say, 'I don't know. I don't know why. Not fully.' I may understand God's overall purposes, but that doesn't mean I have the answer to every question, and an explanation for every occurrence.

I've clung to that classroom reply ever since, in part because I listened in on that exchange just days after I'd been diagnosed with cancer myself.

J. I. Packer put it this way:

> Ought we to be surprised when we find ourselves baffled by what God is doing? No! We must not forget who we are. We are not gods; we are creatures, and no more than creatures. As creatures, we have no right or reason to expect that at every point we shall be able to comprehend the wisdom of our Creator. The King has made it clear to us that it is not his pleasure to disclose all the details of his policy to his human subjects. God has disclosed his mind and will so far as we need to know it for practical

purposes, and we are to take what he has disclosed as a complete and adequate rule for our faith and life. But there will remain things that he has not made known and that, in this life at least, he does not intend us to discover. And the reasons behind God's providential dealings sometimes fall into this category.[2]

These reflections apply on the micro level: that is, why did God bring this or that circumstance to pass? Why didn't he prevent that particular evil I've just heard about—or experienced personally? They also apply on the macro level: that is, why sin and misery at all? Why this kind of world? Why not a different world, a pain-free, suffering-free, wholly happy world?

The Creator replies, 'Creature, will you trust in me, even when you can't explain what I'm up to? Will you embrace what I've been pleased to reveal? Will you walk by faith, and not by the sight that is complete human comprehension?'

It was Abraham who asked the pointed question, 'Shall not the Judge of all the earth do what is just?' (Gen. 18:25). The answer is, he shall. Going all the way back to the formation of his plan in eternity, he always has. As frequently as we ask these questions, his word proves a solid foundation, and a guiding light, every time. There are some things that we cannot understand, but the main things, we can. So let us worship.

---

[2] Cited in 'Knowing and Doing the Will of God,' the devotional for 10 May, drawn from *Hot Tub Religion*, pp. 19-20.

10

FAQs (Cont.): Self-Inflicted Wounds, and Unfriendly Fire

When we turn to consider the human causes of our pains, there are two categories that call for some consideration here. We'll cover two FAQs in this one chapter:

(1) what if my suffering is my own fault?; and

(2) what if I'm hurting because someone else deliberately hurt me?

1. Self-inflicted wounds
What if I'm suffering as a result of my own foolish actions?

I recall this question once coming my way from a visitor to our congregation. At the time he was suffering significant physical ailments that required treatment, and he was persuaded that he'd brought those ailments upon himself by years of foolish dietary habits. He asked me, 'Can I still avail myself of Bible comforts related to suffering when mine is self-inflicted?'

One of the reasons this question comes up is that in Scripture Peter himself emphasizes suffering that is other-inflicted as opposed to self-inflicted—and he puts the latter in its place. Speaking to servants he says, 'For what credit is it if, when you sin and are beaten for it, you endure? But if when you do good and suffer for it you endure, this is a gracious thing in the sight of God' (1 Pet. 2:20). Later in that same letter he says, 'For it is better to suffer for doing good, if that should be God's will, than for doing evil' (3:17).

At first glance this might seem to suggest that if you're suffering the consequences of your own sin, all God says is, 'You deserve it. Deal with it!' But that's just the first glance. Let's take another glance or two. It's certainly true, Peter is highlighting suffering that is other-inflicted, and there is a peculiar and glorious kind of grace that shines when we handle well trials that come upon us as a result of our commitment to Christ. But this doesn't mean the Christian who is suffering as a result of his own folly, and who has repented of that folly, has effectively cut himself off from the Scripture comforts we've covered in this book. Far from it.

Let's take the example of that believer whose body is battling him because he ate badly, carelessly, sinfully, for years. This Christian can still say, God sovereignly appointed that my life should take this turn, including going down into this difficulty and back up again. God was still sovereign even when I was living my life poorly, and treating my body unwisely. This Christian can still say, God appointed this for my good, that I might learn to trust in him, and walk warily of sin in the future. This Christian can still say, in Christ I have a priest and friend who's holding on to me, and forgiving me, and guarding me.

Think about it: if it *were* the case that self-inflicted suffering is entirely beyond the reach of gospel comforts, then we'd be in an awful spiritual predicament! First of all, much of what we suffer in this life *is* the result of our own sin, at least in measure, and some of it is profoundly life-altering. Second of all, we can't fully know the degree to which our sufferings are connected to our sins—ours is a limited vantage point—and we'd be left constantly wondering and guessing and looking for clues and connections and frustrated that we can't find them. Third of all, as we've seen (see chapter 4), in the grand sweep of human history all suffering *is* my own doing—insofar as I stood in Adam my representative when he fell and plunged us all into this mess.

Now, it needs to be said that there are distinctive lessons to be learned when my trials can be traced to my own folly. I should be humbled by this revelation of my frailty, and stirred to make things right in my relationships with those I hurt, and wary about sin going forward. The Westminster Confession of Faith includes this counsel concerning the purposes of God for our wandering, and what results from it:

> The most wise, righteous, and gracious God does often-
> times leave, for a season, his own children to manifold
> temptations, and the corruption of their own hearts, to

chastise them for their former sins, or to discover unto them the hidden strength of corruption and deceitfulness of their hearts, that they may be humbled; and, to raise them to a more close and constant dependence for their support upon himself, and to make them more watchful against all future occasions of sin, and for sundry other just and holy ends (WCF 5.5).

All of those divine purposes (as well as the 'sundry others' that aren't mentioned at the end!) I can embrace as my own, and thus make good use of my falls and their fallout.

2. Unfriendly fire
What if I'm suffering as a result of another person doing me wrong?

This is one of the most poignant subjects when it comes to suffering. 'What if someone else has dealt maliciously with me, so that I'm hurting now, and perhaps scarred for good?' It's even worse, and harder, if that someone seems to be flourishing while you're weeping—maybe even flourishing *because* of what they've done to you. They knocked you down, and now they've scaled new heights by stepping on top of you.

Like our answer to the question right before this one (about self-inflicted suffering), we can begin by saying that the sovereignty, goodness, and grace of God cover this type of suffering too. The Lord reigned when I was wronged, and he still does. And he reigned over me in love, for my eternal good, and he still does. And Christ is my sympathetic friend, and he always will be.[1] Joseph's testimony concerning the way his brothers had wronged him becomes the lens through which we see these things in our own lives: 'As for you, you meant evil against me, but God meant it for good' (Gen. 50:20).

We can add this too: it's perfectly compatible with those truths that in a particular circumstance I might seek earthly justice and recompense for the wrong that was done to me. The apostle Paul sets us an example here. He and Silas were unjustly arrested and brutally beaten in Philippi, and in the aftermath Paul insisted that the governing authorities in that city publicly admit their wrong and vindicate Paul and Silas as Roman citizens (Acts 16:19-40). It takes great wisdom, of course, to know when and how to insist on one's rights in this way, but let no one suggest that suffering as a Christian means that recourse to earthly justice is always sinful.

The Christian who suffers as the result of another's malice finally fixes his eyes on Christ. Peter, urging servants to endure when suffering for doing good, says this:

> For to this you have been called, because Christ also suf-
> fered for you, leaving you an example, so that you might
> follow in his steps. He committed no sin, neither was
> deceit found in his mouth. When he was reviled, he did

---

[1] By the way, I do understand, just to write and read those words—'The Lord reigned when I was wronged'—is to venture into theological territory that for some people is exceedingly painful because of what was done to them. I'm under no illusions. My goal here is simply to set forth the truth that God has revealed for our good, though it may be a long and hard road before a person can rest in that truth, and bless God for it.

> not revile in return; when he suffered, he did not threaten,
> but continued entrusting himself to him who judges justly
> (1 Pet. 2:21-23).

No one—*no one*—was ever wronged as Jesus was. No one ever suffered as Jesus did. And in those awful moments he set us this example: he entrusted himself to his Father in heaven, refraining from vengeance, trusting that his Father would work justice in the end. Jesus' trust shall be vindicated, and so shall ours. Therefore, in the meantime,

> Beloved, never avenge yourselves, but leave it to the wrath
> of God, for it is written, 'Vengeance is mine, I will repay,
> says the Lord.' To the contrary, 'if your enemy is hungry,
> feed him; if he is thirsty, give him something to drink; for
> by so doing you will heap burning coals on his head.' Do
> not be overcome by evil, but overcome evil with good'
> (Rom. 12:19-21).

Just like Jesus, we entrust ourselves to the Father who will overcome evil with good in the end.

11

FAQs (Cont.): What about Viruses and Wildfires?

In the early months of 2020, the global spread of a new respiratory virus brought everyday life in much of the world to a grinding halt. Soon everyone was wondering about this disease called COVID-19 and dealing with its life-altering repercussions: events cancelled, schools closed, businesses shuttered, whole communities locked down. It loomed large in the news, and in people's lives, and in their hearts and minds—in part because this sort of suffering now looked to be a new normal. Even as communities and countries were battling that particular virus, they were already bracing for the next one. It was a potent brew of loss and change, fear and uncertainty, isolation and polarization. And in its potency it seemed to bring out the best and worst in humanity at the very same time.

COVID-19 and how to handle it became a FAQ for the church almost overnight, and it stayed that way. We might even say, an *EAQ*: an 'Emotionally Asked Question.' So many died from COVID, and so many painful disruptions resulted from it, and so many deep fears and divisions were fuelled by it, it's no wonder the Christian church wrestled with it, and mightily. Even the church's gatherings for worship on Sundays were impacted.

The goal in this chapter isn't to offer up epidemiological reflections. (Good thing, too: I'm decidedly unqualified for that!) Rather, it's to highlight truths from God's word that help us to interpret trials of this character: suffering that sweeps across regions and nations and even around the world, washing indiscriminately over our common humanity in wave after wave. Viruses come and go, and then a different one follows, but the word of our God stands forever. Let's consider the answers it provides.

1. Nothing new under the Sun

The first point to make is to underline something we just noticed in passing: that is, there is something perennial about this type of trial. Look back over history: this isn't unprecedented. In 1918–1920, it was the Great Influenza. In the fourteenth century, it was the Bubonic Plague. And of course it's not just the big ones way back when. There's a reason COVID-19 has the '19' in it: respiratory viruses emerge and spread with such frequency that they're sometimes labelled according to the year they were discovered, so as to distinguish them from those that came before and after. Throw in floods and droughts and wildfires, and the point becomes clearer.

God's word helps us to understand this. As we've already noticed (back in chapter 4), God justly imposed a curse upon creation after our fall into sin, so that life here on planet earth would be marked by difficulty and disease, decay and death. All of these plagues and viruses and floods and wildfires that we experience in our own time, they serve as reminders that the curse remains. They also remind us of our connectedness as a single human race of embodied creatures: our good God made us body and soul, and made us one human race. Sadly, under the curse, that means we can suffer as one race too. We are fearfully and wonderfully made (Psa. 139:14), both individually and corporately, but that implies we can be fearfully devastated as well. The point is, none of these things have changed. Until Jesus returns, they never will. That doesn't mean we give up trying to find solutions and best practices when it comes to pandemics and the like. It just means we maintain perspective, and keep our balance.

2. *It's complicated*

Our foolish propensity when we confront some trying circumstance (especially one that's worldwide in scope) is to do so in a way that's reductionistic. We want to focus on just one aspect, and analyze the situation in terms of just one cause, so that we can blame just one factor—or person. How convenient. But under the curse these things are complicated. Suffering can be messy, involving so many different coloured threads all tangled up in a ball. It's true that nature itself is against us now (Gen. 3:17, 18), but it's also true that human beings make wise and foolish decisions as those who live together in this natural world, and those decisions matter. Winds spread a wildfire, but it may be a fool in a campsite who started it. A tsunami rises from the ocean, but it may be the lack of a proper warning system that compounds the death toll. A virus makes its way into a country unbidden, and can spread through the most ordinary, innocent human interaction, but then it takes human wisdom, creativity, and perseverance to respond to it.

We honour the Lord when we practice the kind of patience that surveys the sweep of a complicated circumstance (though that's harder, naturally), including factors local and global, causes natural and human, actions innocent and otherwise, seeking humbly and patiently to learn and understand, and willing to receive correction when correction is called for. 'The one who states his case first seems right, until the other comes and examines him' (Prov. 18:17). Sometimes we need that other person to examine our view of a matter before we realize that our take didn't take in quite enough. When global suffering overwhelms us, it's natural to latch on to a quick and easy interpretation of it all, but that's not the way to go.

3. *Repent or perish*
In Luke 13, Jesus reflects upon the deaths of some who were killed under Pilate, and others who were crushed by a falling tower in Jerusalem. In his interpretation he lays the emphasis not where many of his contemporaries would

have wanted. Instead of trying to find a way to blame those individuals for the fate they suffered, Jesus turns it into a pointed word for everyone: 'unless you repent, you will all likewise perish' (verses 3, 5).

This reminds us where our own emphasis ought to be found. There's nothing wrong with wanting to understand (insofar as we can) the causes and effects that may be at work in a given situation, including an epidemiological one. In many circumstances that kind of analysis is positively vital. And though we have to tread carefully here, that may even include considering the responsibility borne by those who are suffering in some way. But ultimately we have to read these moments as signs: they remind us that the worldwide curse we're living under now is just, and that we have to turn back to God in order to be delivered from the wrath to come (1 Thess. 1:10)—a fate we all deserve. We may not be able to sort out all the factors that contribute to this or that earthly calamity, but we can be certain about this: those calamities rightly put us on notice that, apart from saving grace, we're all sinners in the hands of an angry God, and gospel repentance is the remedy.

Here too we see these situations are complex, not just in terms of natural causes but also with respect to their spiritual significance. One and the same calamity comes to those in God's family as a trial from their loving Father meant to advance their eternal good, but to those cut off from that family it comes as a fearful reminder that wrath is real and on its way. Think of it this way: it's one sign, but the sign has writing on both sides.

4. We're being watched

Whenever some form of suffering comes along that impacts whole communities at once, Christians and non-Christians alike, the church needs to bear in mind that the world is watching how she responds. The people of God bear a solemn responsibility to show their neighbours what it looks like to suffer with faith, hope, and love, especially because everyone's caught up in the same circumstance.

So the question becomes, what will others see in us? Will they see faith, which holds on to Scripture so as to be steadied in the storm, and calls others to join us? Will they see hope, which looks forward to the world to come, so as not to be undone in this one? Will they see love? Love for our neighbours, by reaching out in tangible service, and seeking ways to live well with our fellow citizens in a trying time? Or will they see us absorbed only with ourselves, embracing an 'every man for himself' mentality? And will they see us practicing love for one another in the church? Or will they see us Christians biting and devouring one another (in the name of Jesus, even) over differences in opinion about civil and churchly policy? May it never be.

COVID became the great FAQ in 2020, but this kind of suffering we shall always have with us, and the questions that go along with it. Thank God for his word, where answers are to be found. May the church show herself to be a people who have embraced them.

12

The End

The best thing about this book on suffering is that it's about to end.

Suffering, I mean. Not the book.

Though the book is too. We're entering the home stretch.

In this chapter we turn our attention to the truth for which our souls have been aching from the beginning, namely, the sure promise that one day God's people will suffer no more.

One range, two peaks

When it comes to the heavenly future that Christians have in store, it's important to bear in mind that ours is a double-horizon hope. Gaze out on the mountain range that is our future in Christ, and two grand peaks meet your gaze, one nearer than the other. In the foreground is the prospect of going to be with Christ in heaven right away through death, the soul welcomed into that world above while the body remains here, laid to rest. (See Phil. 1:22-24, where Paul admits to feeling 'hard pressed': 'My desire is to depart and be with Christ, for that is far better. But to remain in the flesh is more necessary on your account.') In the background is a more distant, and yet more glorious peak, which is the prospect of Jesus' return at the end of this age to inaugurate the world to come, including the resurrection of our bodies (Phil. 3:20, 21: from heaven 'we await a Saviour, the Lord Jesus Christ, who will transform our lowly body to be like his glorious body') and the glorification of planet earth (Rom. 8:21: 'the creation itself will be set free from its bondage to corruption and obtain the freedom of the glory of the children of God').

One range, two peaks.

To reach that first summit (that is, the one in the foreground, going to be with Christ through death) will surely mean unprecedented blessedness for the Christian personally. In that unimaginable moment, it must be that the believer is made perfect in holiness, finally and entirely set free from all sin, and welcomed into Jesus' very presence, and the presence of those who have gone before. And yet it's still true that those who are there, holy and happy in this way, are also aware that their fellow believers still suffer on earth, including the pains of persecution, and that they themselves—even in heaven—don't yet experience the full salvation Christ gained for them.

Remember, even though they're in heaven, they're still experiencing death, for they're still in a state of the separation of soul from body (the Bible calls them 'the *dead* in Christ,' 1 Thess. 4:16). This is why they can be heard crying out, 'O Sovereign Lord, holy and true, how long?'

(Rev. 6:10). How long until you end all wrong and make all things right? They cry out like this 'with a loud voice,' not because they remain pained in heaven as they were on earth, but because they long for the completion of what remains unfinished, including the vindication of the justice of God. Precisely because they are brothers and sisters in a spiritual family that spans the cosmos in time and space, and because they know Christ is a Saviour who saves 'to the uttermost' (Heb. 7:25), they can't feel totally satisfied until the whole church has been wholly rescued and raised, and their Father's name totally hallowed. That day is coming.

At the end of the Bible we're given a glimpse of it. In the book of Revelation the apostle John describes the vision he's given of 'a new heaven and a new earth' which God has in store for us, and John also relays the word he hears to accompany that vision:

> He will wipe away every tear from their eyes, and death shall be no more, neither shall there be mourning, nor crying, nor pain anymore, for the former things have passed away (Rev. 21:4).

Finally, no more suffering for the redeemed people of God.

When it says 'the former things have passed away,' this doesn't mean the world to come will bear no resemblance to this one whatsoever, and carry no connection with it. Remember, Jesus' promise is that the meek shall inherit the earth (Matt. 5:5), not stand back and watch it get obliterated and replaced, just as Paul teaches that the created order is longing for its own liberation, not its annihilation (Rom.

8:19-21). This turns out to be an important truth when it comes to suffering: the pains and problems we experience in this life do not belong essentially to earthly, embodied experience. It's not the human body, and rocks and trees and water and fire, that are to blame. Rather, as we've seen before, our trials can be traced back to the curse that now rests upon creation. Thus our hope is the lifting of that curse, so that creation shines after all. (Glorified rocks and trees!) This is one of the reasons why our suffering in this age makes us groan (as Paul puts it in that same Romans 8 passage): deep down we have a sense that earthly, embodied life doesn't have to be like this, and wasn't meant to be like this, and won't be like this forever. What a glorious day that will be, the long-expected day of—*Liberation!*

Perhaps most remarkably, even Jesus himself is described as waiting for that day:

> But when Christ had offered for all time a single sacrifice for sins, he sat down at the right hand of God, waiting from that time until his enemies should be made a footstool for his feet (Heb. 10:12, 13).

Death itself, the ultimate earthly curse, is one of those enemies (1 Cor. 15:25, 26), and therefore so must be all the suffering his people have had to endure.

Thanks to our experience in this life, in which our waiting is so often mixed with impatience and inactivity and doubt, in part because we're not in control, it's hard for us to imagine Christ waiting for anything at all. But he is waiting, and he's doing so with perfect patience, even as he royally reigns from heaven and actively builds his church on earth, and he's doing so with unshakeable confidence that the final day will come and his expectations will not be dashed. That very thought has the effect of vindicating and fuelling our own longing for the same day.

Free at last

The prospect of the end of suffering in the world to come proves especially comforting for Christians who face trials in this life that seem positively irreversible. And in some cases they don't just 'seem' to be. They are.

It could be the Christian whose body is permanently paralyzed as the result of an accident. It might be the believer who suffers from some form of mental illness. It could be the Christian whose memory is permanently scarred as a result of abuse during childhood. Or consider our brothers and sisters in Christ who this very day face profound fears and daunting obstacles simply because of the colour of their skin, and who must wonder after hundreds of years of racism and injustice if anything like a new day will ever dawn.

True, in some of these cases progress is possible, and change should be sought for and fought for. 'Let us not grow weary of doing good' (Gal. 6:9), including the good of trying to make things better for ourselves and others, personally and socially. But when the roots of our suffering reach deep, deep down into the hard soil of this cursed world, far beneath the reach of our own goodness, wisdom, and power, it's no wonder we find ourselves aching for the day when the God of infinite goodness and unsearchable wisdom and almighty power will reach down and do the uprooting himself. And he will. Abraham asked, 'Shall not the Judge of all the earth do what is just?' (Gen. 18:25). Yes, Abraham. Yes he will. And it will indeed be an act of divine justice (as well as faithfulness and mercy) for God to make all things right in the end, since Jesus gained a complete salvation for us by his life and death, and the Father must have a right regard for his Son's saving sacrifice. Whether it's damage to our bodies, minds, and relationships that truly is irreversible in this life, or social brokenness that seems perennial, or anything in between, in the end we shall be free at last. Free from all of it.

Will we remember?

One of the questions that crosses our minds as we ponder the prospect of heaven (here's another FAQ!) is whether we'll have any memory there of what we experienced here, including our suffering. We've already noticed there will be some continuity that connects our experience in this life and the life to come. The question is, will there be the continuity of memory as well?

It would be unrealistic to suggest that in the world to come we'll have no memory whatsoever of the fact that we suffered in this one (though of course we can't know now how complete, and how detailed, that memory will be). After all, we'll love Christ in that world as the one who *saved* us, which means we'll remember in some fashion that we were a people who needed to be saved, saved from sin and misery. That reality will not have been erased entirely from our memory banks. Sometimes in this life we hope it *will* be erased, and we have a hard time imagining that heaven will be truly heavenly if it hasn't been. But that's because our only experience of memory is the way it works in this life, in which Christ is physically removed far from us and memories can cause us pain. When it comes to the idea of heavenly memory, we need to walk by faith and not by sight, and not allow our sense of what's possible in the coming age to be limited to what we've always known in this one. Whatever we do remember about our sufferings, we will remember it as those who gaze upon the glory of God in the face of Jesus—I mean, physically face-to-face!—and who are filled with joy to the point of overflowing at the thought that God in Jesus set us free. Here too, we need not fear. We can trust that our God knows how to bring it about that our memories will make for worship and joy—even if it's difficult for us to grasp it now.

The perseverance of the (hopeful) saints

Until that day, our calling as Christians is to hope for that world, and to let that rock solid, anchor-for-the-soul hope (Heb. 6:19) encourage us to press on and persevere in the Lord's service.

The apostle Peter helps us here. It's no wonder that Peter has so much to say about the church's heavenly hope in a letter (1 Peter) in which the church's suffering is a major theme, especially due to the world's opposition. Peter rejoices that God 'has caused us to be born again to a living hope through the resurrection of Jesus Christ from the dead' (1:3). (See also 1:13 and 3:15.) He says these things to people who are opposed and maligned for their faith and faithfulness (for example, those who don't know God 'speak against you as evildoers,' 2:12), and by extension we can apply them to our sufferings of all sorts. From a mere human vantage point, and relying merely upon human resources, any people who find themselves weighed down and beaten down have no good cause for hopefulness in a hopeless world. It doesn't make sense that they should keep going. And yet hopeful and persevering is what we are! This is exactly why Christians need to be ready to explain themselves ('always being prepared to make a defence to anyone who asks you for a reason for the hope that is in you,' 3:15). They don't need to wear T-shirts that say, 'Ask me why I'm hopeful.' Ideally their very lives send that signal, and raise the question. 'Why do your lives have a far-away look? And why do you insist on holding on to a faith that seems to cause you so much trouble?'

Once more, here we look to Christ as the pioneer who led the way. Jesus himself remembers what it meant to make the most of hope when he was suffering. And that's why we're called to fix our gaze on him now. We're to 'run with endurance the race that is set before us,' and we're to do so 'looking to Jesus, the founder and perfecter of our faith, who for the joy that was set before him endured the cross, despising the shame, and is seated at the right hand of the throne of God' (Heb. 12:1, 2). Here on earth, when he was that Suffering Servant and Man of Sorrows, he set his hope fully on the joy in store, and he knew about that joy because he knew his Father's word. And that makes his footsteps the perfect ones for us to follow.

Conclusion

It's easy to caricature this message of heavenly hope to those suffering on earth as a 'pie in the sky' distraction. No doubt it's been abused that way by some, as a way of lulling the downtrodden into acquiescence and thus preserving systems and structures that benefit the few at the expense of the many. But let's not allow that abuse to cause us to set these sweet truths aside! It's perfectly consistent that we should strive for earthly good, including the alleviation of suffering, at the same time that we long for the world to come. And not only is it consistent, it's positively connected: it's that hopeful heavenly prospect that keeps us going here on earth, pouring ourselves into callings of all sorts, enduring and addressing pains along the way.

Pie in the sky? Hardly. I for one can't wait to sample the desserts in the eschatological banquet on glorified solid ground. Jesus endured for the joy set before him. His joy will be made complete when we feast with him, and so will ours.

13

Practical Counsels

In our first twelve chapters we covered a wide sweep of Bible truth. Here at the conclusion we pivot slightly and turn our attention to some practical counsels. How might we take the truths we've surveyed in this book and take them with us into everyday living? Some parting words pointing to life application.

1. Stop and think

Paul says to the Colossians, 'Let the word of Christ dwell in you richly' (Col. 3:16), and that's a good place for us to start here. It may seem like a 'needless to say,' but it needs to be said! All the truth we covered in the chapters leading to this one, we need to get that truth into our minds, and via our minds into our hearts. And that doesn't happen automatically. That takes meditation. The truly blessed man is the one whose 'delight is in the law of the LORD, and on his law he meditates day and night' (Psa. 1:2). You can read every book on this subject there is to be read (and there are a lot of them), and keep pages and pages of sermon notes you took over the years, but have you ever stopped to think about any of it, and to reflect upon your own heart and ways in the light of it? It's one of the great misconceptions of our time, the notion that simply being inundated with information means you've processed it and are making good use of it. So go for a walk, and do some of that processing. Ask yourself, if I had to sum up in my own words some key Bible truths related to suffering, how would I put it? For example, how would I express the truth of God's sovereignty to someone who's struggling with that idea? Or, how might I articulate the purposes for which God brings trials into our lives? Or, how might I point to Christ as the pioneer who went first? Your own words. Words that draw upon your own experiences. And then ask yourself, which of those truths have I had a hard time with personally? And then ask the Lord for grace to receive what he's said in his word, because he *is* gracious, just like that.

Which brings us to—

2. Don't wait

The time to do that processing I just described—is *now*. Don't wait. Don't wait until you find yourself in the crucible of suffering before you start to ponder and pray over these things. By all means, God is able to reorient our thinking in remarkable and dramatic ways in the midst of trials. And some Christians do have stories like that to tell: 'God used a devastating episode to change my thinking—my thinking about him, and about myself, and about his purposes—and to change it radically.' But all things being equal, isn't it preferable to have those truths deeply rooted now, so that you already have them in hand when you enter the valley in the first place? Yes, it's possible to learn new things in less-than-ideal circumstances, but (looking back to 2020 again) there's good reason why, when in-person schooling was limited or halted altogether, students and parents and teachers and school administrators all found themselves longing for a return to 'normal' learning. (Well, many students anyway.) In some settings it's just easier to concentrate, and consider, and even collaborate with fellow learners.

C. S. Lewis was right to say that learning ought to continue in wartime, but we can also say that learning is easier in peacetime. And that's true spiritually as well. When the storms of suffering and strife are already beating against our walls and windows, violently, relentlessly, that's not the best time to begin thinking about God's sovereignty, and his purposes, and his Son. Go for that walk now, while it's sunny outside. Because it won't stay that way.

Which brings us to—

3. Teach your children well

The children of our churches, including the little churches that are our homes, need to hear these truths taught clearly, and see them modelled practically. Here too we can say, don't wait! The time to train them in this way begins early on, long before they'll fully understand all that life in this world entails. Even when the trials they're facing are skinned knees and broken toys and rained-out play dates, the shepherding can and ought to be underway.

It is a sobering realization, I know, to consider that we're bringing our children up in a world of such sorrow—and that they themselves won't be untouched by it. That realization hit me hard as a father one day when our children were little, and I took them to a park near our house. Picture perfect day. Brilliant warm sun. Clear blue sky. My children happy and healthy and swinging in the swings while I nudged them gently into the air, making them smile, and I was smiling with them. It was a time when I'd been pondering as a pastor the truths we've covered now in this book, truths about suffering and how to handle it in Christ. It seemed so incongruous: this beautiful, blissful, sunlit family scene against the backdrop of those hard truths about life's storms, both present and future. It was as if I could look off into the horizon, and see where the clear blue sky gave way to threatening clouds.

In those moments I could see things that my children could not. I remember thinking, *My dear children, you have no idea what this world is like that your mother and I have brought you into, and none of us has any way of knowing what the valleys will be that you'll have to go down into personally.* And when it hits you that you're going to bring them up to follow Christ, which will mean that added layer of opposition and strife and self-denial, then the realization becomes all the more real.

But that only reinforces the imperative to train them, after all. Whether it's the things we teach them around the dining table and in by-the-way conversations in the car, or the way we pray for them when they're hurting, or the way we handle our own trials as our children are watching us (and make no mistake, they *are* watching us), we hand over to them the truths we've surveyed in these chapters, especially the truth of our suffering in union with Christ. And we hand those truths over to them as the stuff of life. We don't give our children mere ideas and abstractions: we give them the faith that was once for all delivered to the saints, marked now with our fingerprints and stained with our tears, but solid as a rock, and therefore able to hold them up when they're weeping too.

Which brings us to—

4. *Live like a church member*

One of the most important practical counsels we can consider when it comes to our trials is that we dare not walk hard roads alone. When Peter wants to encourage suffering Christians to resist the Evil One and stand firm, he says they should do so 'knowing that the same kinds of suffering are being experienced by your brotherhood throughout the world' (1 Pet. 5:9). This is a principle we can apply to our troubles across the board: solidarity matters. It matters on a global scale, as Peter implies. We belong to a worldwide body that's ever forged by affliction. It also matters on the local level: God gathers his people into churches where they share in one another's lives and pains. God's purpose for the church is 'that there may be no division in the body, but that the members may have the same care for one another. If one member suffers, all suffer together; if one member is honoured, all rejoice together' (1 Cor. 12:25, 26).

This partnership pays off in a variety of 'P's.

(i) Perspective

When I'm knit together with fellow believers who are burdened in their own ways, whether similar to mine or not, I'm reminded that this is what God's children experience in this life. 'The LORD reproves him whom he loves, as a father the son in whom he delights' (Prov. 3:12). Left entirely to myself, staring out the window with no one else around, I can easily drift into thinking that God has abandoned me. I can lose perspective. But when I look around in the worship service (and other churchly settings) and see that mine aren't the only cheeks that are tear-stained, I'm brought back to my senses, back to resting in the knowledge of God's love.

(ii) Prayer

The Lord says about his church, 'My house shall be called a house of prayer for all peoples' (Isa. 56:7). The fact that Jesus got so angry to discover that his fellow Jews had lost sight of that (Matt. 21:13) reminds us just how important prayer is as an aspect of church life. And praying for one another in the midst of suffering is particularly powerful. These days it's become commonplace in the wider culture to disparage expressions like 'We're sending so-and-so our thoughts and prayers in their time of sorrow.' Frankly, there's a measure of truth in that disparagement: some people do throw those expressions around without meaning them (not unlike the post-sneeze 'God bless you'), and the very idea of 'sending prayers' to another person is rather strange, to say the least. (Especially when it's combined with sending them 'good vibrations'!) But let's not allow disparagement and insincerity and poor word choices to cause us, as the church, to shrink back from the wonderful gift of prayer. When I'm weighed down in some way, to know that fellow believers are lifting me up to the Lord means the world. Even more so if I'm with them at the time, and we've gone to God's throne together, and I'm hearing their prayers for me live and in person. A precious gift.

(iii) Practical service

When we're done praying, we get up off our knees and we get to work. In other words, heartfelt prayer for those suffering in the church goes hand in hand with practical service to meet their needs, both spiritual and physical. This is an aspect of what we call 'the communion of the saints': fellow church members are 'knit together in love' (Col. 2:2), and that love shows in the way we care for another. Indeed, insofar as we close our hearts against brothers and sisters in need, it can be fairly asked if the love of God truly abides in us in the first place (1 John 3:17).

And remember, this mutual service in the body works both ways: each Christian is both giver and receiver. Whenever we welcome a new member into the congregation I pastor, one of the encouragements we give to the church is this: 'Allow this new member a place of service in your lives.' Counter-intuitive, perhaps? Christians usually think of their responsibility solely in the other direction: 'I'm called to serve others.' And that's certainly part of it. But it's not the whole of it. Another aspect of church life is letting others serve me. Paul urges the Galatians, 'Bear one another's burdens, and so fulfil the law of Christ' (Gal. 6:2). If you try to go it alone and shoulder your burdens all by yourself when they're plainly too much for you to bear, you're effectively denying your fellow church members the opportunity to fulfil Christ's law. And there's nothing heroic about that.

Which brings us, finally, to—

5. How to comfort

I've been asked many times for advice about how to comfort those who are suffering. I only have space here to offer a few counsels, but hopefully these will serve as a good start.

(i) Just do it

Sometimes we allow the thought of our own inadequacy as comforters to freeze us, so that we don't reach out, lest we say the wrong words to someone who's in pain, and mess things up, and make it more painful. But that only keeps us from offering the comforts we do have to give. Might you say some wrong words, or offer a clumsy gesture? Absolutely. Reach out anyway. Being a wise comforter takes (you guessed it) wisdom, and wisdom takes time and experience and even a little trial-and-error. Think of the most impressively compassionate person you know, someone who always seems to know what to say and not to say, and how to help, and how to listen. It's a near 100% certainty they could tell you stories of times they said the wrong thing, or missed an opportunity, or meddled where they didn't belong.

This doesn't mean it's okay to be careless. Yes, give some thought beforehand to what you might say, and how you might help. Seek out advice from those who have been in this person's shoes. Reflect upon your own experience. Those are all good, wise pre-steps. Especially if the person you want to comfort is suffering something particularly painful. But don't allow the possibility that the practice of compassion will feel awkward or uncertain to hold you back. The church is a family where brothers and sisters sometimes blunder, but grace abounds, and wisdom is gained.

Just do it.

(ii) Never underestimate the gift of listening

As a preacher and writer I know well the temptation to think that the speaking of many words will cure all ills and remove all sorrows. Alas, it isn't so. Sometimes the most timely and treasured service we can render is simply to *be* with another person who's hurting, and to hear them out, even if they don't have words right now either, and all we're hearing is their silence too. God has said much in his word about suffering, but that doesn't mean we have to say something every time. Or maybe words are called for, but they're words about football, or films, or what you did on Friday. You're going for a walk with someone who has cancer, but cancer may be the last thing they want to talk about. Or maybe you touch on it briefly and move on, just long enough to give them an opening to go there if that's what they want.

And you don't have to give them a book either! This author happily admits there are times when giving somebody a book to read is not the way to go. Well-intentioned, perhaps, but ill-advised. Maybe ask first: 'Do you like to read? Would you enjoy a book or an article if I come across something that makes me think of you?' Never hurts to ask.

(iii) Commune with Christ the Comforter

This is a concluding practical counsel, to be sure—but admittedly it's also an excuse to come back to our union with Christ one more time before the book is done.

As we've seen several times in these pages, in Jesus Christ we have a sympathetic high priest who comforts us now with the same prospect of everlasting joy that once comforted him in the face of the cross. Do you want to be a compassionate Christian in the midst of fellow believers around you? Then fix your eyes on Christ. Spend time with him. Get to know him. Read his word. Talk to him. That goes for the church as a whole. A congregation whose life and ministry are centred around the sufferings and glories of Christ is far more likely to be a community where people weep with those who weep, and bear one another's burdens in practical ways.

Jesus led the way. He cares for his own. He envelops us with his grace. And he points us forward to the coming Day.

> After you have suffered a little while, the God of all grace, who has called you to his eternal glory in Christ, will himself restore, confirm, strengthen, and establish you. To him be the dominion forever and ever. Amen (1 Pet. 5:10, 11).

Further Reading

Where to start

Dan McCartney, *Why Does It Have to Hurt? The Meaning of Christian Suffering* (Phillipsburg, NJ: P&R Publishing, 1998)

R. C. Sproul, *Surprised by Suffering: The Role of Pain and Death in the Christian Life* (Sanford, FL: Reformation Trust Publishing, 2009)

In more detail

D. A. Carson, *How Long, O Lord? Reflections on Suffering and Evil* (Ada, MI: Baker Academic, 1991)

Sinclair Ferguson, *Deserted by God?* (Edinburgh: Banner of Truth Trust, 1996)

Nancy Guthrie, ed., *Be Still, My Soul: Embracing God's Purpose and Provision in Suffering* (Wheaton, IL: Crossway, 2010)

Joni Eareckson Tada, *Songs of Suffering: 25 Hymns and Devotions for Weary Souls* (Wheaton, IL: Crossway, 2022)

Mark Talbot, *Suffering and the Christian Life*, 2 vols (Wheaton, IL: Crossway, 2020)

Robert A. Peterson, *Hell on Trial: The Case for Eternal Punishment* (Phillipsburg, NJ: P&R Publishing, 1995)

Kim Riddlebarger, *A Case for Amillennialism: Understanding the End Times* (Ada, MI: Baker Books and Leicester: Inter-Varsity Press, 2003)

Cornelis P. Venema, *The Promise of the Future* (Edinburgh: Banner of Truth Trust, 2000)

The bigger picture

Thomas Boston, *The Crook in the Lot* (Edinburgh: Banner of Truth Trust, 2017)

John Calvin, *The Golden Booklet of the True Christian Life* (Ada, MI: Baker Books, 1975)

Richard Gaffin, *Resurrection and Redemption: A Study in Paul's Soteriology* (Phillipsburg, NJ: P&R Publishing, 2000)

Samuel Rutherford, *The Letters of Samuel Rutherford* (Edinburgh: Banner of Truth Trust, 2006)

Thomas Watson, *All Things for Good* (Edinburgh: Banner of Truth Trust, 1986)